Lord, Please Make Him Stop Drinking

Lord, Please Make Him STOP DRINKING

The Christian Woman's Guide to Thrive No Matter What

CHRISTINE LENNARD FOLK

NEW YORK

LONDON • NASHVILLE • MELBOURNE • VANCOUVER

Lord, Please Make Him Stop Drinking

The Christian Woman's Guide to Thrive No Matter What

Published in New York, New York, by Morgan James Publishing. Morgan James is a trademark of Morgan James, LLC. www.MorganJamesPublishing.com

ISBN 9781642797770 paperback
ISBN 9781642797787 eBook
Library of Congress Control Number: 2019913824

Cover Design by:
Rachel Lopez
www.r2cdesign.com

Interior Design by:
Christopher Kirk
www.GFSstudio.com

Morgan James is a proud partner of Habitat for Humanity Peninsula and Greater Williamsburg. Partners in building since 2006.

Get involved today! Visit
MorganJamesPublishing.com/giving-back

Dedicated to Jesus Christ

Table of Contents

CHAPTER 1

Are You Frustrated?

It's happened again. You can't believe it. He fell off the wagon...again and there you are sitting in your car trying to decide if you should just go get a hotel for the night...again or wait it out for a while. He'll eventually slow down and pass out on the couch.

The reality is you're married. You made a vow to your Heavenly Father and your husband all those years ago. You admit that you had an inkling there were issues before you said, "I do." How could you have known it would escalate to this? You know God is going to use all this turmoil for good, for His glory.

"But when? When will he hit his bottom? When will he turn to you, Lord? If only he loved me more than the bottle. How can I possibly survive his drunken tirade one more time, let alone for the rest of my life?"

"Lord, what can I do? Please give me the hope that this is not how I will live out my life. What can I do or say that will make him stop drinking or at least stop treating me like I'm the worst piece of crap!?"

God loves you and He does not want you to live like this for the rest of your life. He wants your husband to treat you with kindness and respect. He wants you to have peace in your home.

You are about to be introduced to keys that will unlock the big doors that have been blocking you from having the promises God has made to you—having His love, peace, His Joy, and abundance no matter how your husband shows up—drunk, not drunk, or wanting to drink. These keys will be yours from now on and no matter what he does. Your husband won't be able to steal your connection to these gifts.

This Book Is for You:

- If your husband makes you feel defeated, angry, and even hopeless sometimes.
- If you are having that same tired argument with your husband over and over again; he just won't listen to you; he won't do things like he used to.
- If he is angry all the time and you're embarrassed because you handle him so poorly, not like a Christian.

- If you feel God's word and prayer is not helping.
- If you go a long time without touching, or talking.
- If you don't spend any time with each other.
- If you are punishing him with the silent treatment or he is punishing you with the silent treatment.
- If you feel disrespected; you get the sense he doesn't love you and at times he hates you.
- If you can't sleep at night as your mind just won't stop thinking.
- If you just don't understand how God's word applies to your situation.
- If you feel something is blocking you from getting what you want or from hearing from God to know what you should do.
- If you would like to respond like Jesus would to your alcoholic husband.
- If you would like to transform the nasty parts of your relationship.

Lord, Please Make Him Stop Drinking will give you the tools you need to know exactly what you need to do to make your marriage survivable until God transforms it.

It's Not a Coincidence

Here's what I know: you wouldn't be reading this book if God hadn't put it in your hands. It's hard to seek help and advice about an alcoholic husband. If you read this book and make an ongoing effort to learn and practice what's in it, then you'll have exactly what you need to change what he says and how often he gets away with it for rest of your life, all the while being a collaborator with your best buddy, Jesus.

You have a choice here between living with the frustration of being a victim to his drinking cycles, allowing him to erode your self-esteem or living with the victory of Christ in your heart to change your marriage.

This information centers around your communication with Christ and applying God's Word so that when your husband shows up drunk, he meets Jesus in you instead of you. Most twelve step programs start by admitting you are powerless. I had two counselors tell me I should get a divorce. Maybe it's because it's the easier path, but I've come to know that the Power of Jesus and the wisdom of His Word transforms crappy disrespectful drunken conflict into understanding, love, and peace.

You have read inspirational stories and self-help books, gone to counseling or Al-Anon, maybe talked to your pastor and confided in your friends, and fasted. You have prayed and prayed, read God's Word over and over again. You know the answer is in there because you've experienced His transformation. He has rescued you and synchronized circumstances that made things work out in amazing ways. Everything that you've experienced has had to have happened before this book got to you so that it could make the impact in your heart it needed to.

Lots of Christian women wallow in despair for so long they're depressed, their backs are killing them, disease has set in, or they turn to another man, or to food, to "religion" or work. We think, "Lord, why does it have to be like this?"

It's taken me a long time to grab hold of all the "Keys to the Kingdom" that you are about to learn. I've been working with clients and teaching these keys since 2007. From my years of being married to an angry alcoholic and trying to apply my faith to the problem, I've learned that I can change the circumstances and people around me. Christ did. And you are about to, too!

God knows you tried. If your husband could have been changed with all the stuff you know and all the stuff you've done up to this point, surely, he would have stopped drinking by now.

I came to understand all that experience was necessary. God was refining me like a silversmith refines silver.

"He will sit as a smelter and purifier of silver."
–Malachi 3:3a

Our "Silversmith" carefully holds the silver in the center of the fire where the flames are hottest in order to burn away all the impurities. The Silversmith must not only stay in front of the fire the whole time, but He must keep His eyes on the silver the entire time because if the silver is left a moment too long in the flames, it would be destroyed. The moment our Silversmith sees His reflection in the purified silver it is immediately removed from the fire. Take comfort knowing that He has His eyes on you right now. He is holding you. He knows you are in pain, frustrated, and confused about all this turmoil you've had to endure.

The Lord has shown me how to keep my eyes on Him while I'm in the fire. The decisions you make when you're in the fire affect your outcome and the outcome for your husband. If the outcome you want is to transform all your suffering, your tears, and disappointment into something you could not only survive in, but thrive in, then keep reading. Your marriage has lasted too long, struggled too much, to let the love you started out with be extinguished.

The first thing we have to do is take care of your heart. If you're not absolutely sure Christ lives in you, if you haven't spent much time with Him lately, or spoken to Him in a while, just ask Him, "Lord Jesus, please enter my heart and stay there even when I'm not thinking about you. You are my Lord and Savior."

That's a great start. To have clarity and joy and courage to work out your relationship with your husband you have to start with Christ as your Foundation.

This book has many doors of wisdom that we will be unlocking with keys from scripture. The good news is it's not as big as the Bible, so the best way to use this book is to read it through cover to cover. You'll want to stop as your jaw drops as the simple, profound practices keep unfolding. Just keep reading because I need to give you a picture of how all of these keys work together. It's a process (I cover this in my course). Once you see all the doors of wisdom lined up together, you'll be able to use the book more as a reference guide. When you identify when you're stuck and things aren't changing; or you find you are arguing with him; and you feel you've lost your connection to God, come back to the book and find the examples and ideas that will help you work through it. Remember there is always a breakdown before a breakthrough.

It's important for you to know that the scripture in this book took years for me to unlock. You've read them so many times and wondered why you don't have what Christ promised, *"That they may have life and have it abundantly."* (John 10:10) Just reading through this book once is not going to unlock all those doors of transforming wisdom. The keys are in here, but it's your decision to make. Do the work, make the notes, highlight the epiphanies when you find the right key.

If you don't currently have a prayer journal, I highly recommend it as you read through this book. Rewrite some of the key points and scriptures discussed in your own words applying the concepts to you and what you are experiencing. The more you do this you'll feel more connected to God and to the leading of the Holy Spirit so you can do God's will—not yours.

This all starts with you.

As your teacher or communications coach, I can't do any of this program for you. When I was in the midst of despair, driving around wondering where I could go until my husband came down from his temper tantrum, I would think about someday having a beautiful Victorian place overlooking Little Travers Bay with a big wraparound porch, gardens, and a beautiful view where Christian wives and their children could get away from the anger and yelling and name calling. God wanted me to go through all that misery so that He could help you, not just for a couple of nights, but for the rest of your life. It's up to you to make the decision to do this program for you. For your sanity, for peace in your home. Once you see how he stops yelling and you notice he is ranting less often, you'll know this book was in your hands for a life-changing reason.

This book is filled with scripture, of course. His word is how I finally overcame the obstacles that Satan was using to destroy me—destroy my clients. God made connections with me through His Word. Your faith and your relationship with your husband will grow to be more Christ-like as you integrate these keys. By rereading pages that aren't clicking for you, doing worksheets on what you need clarified, or sharing your process with your husband and others who want what they see you now have, before long you'll know exactly what God is trying to tell you and you won't get goaded into arguing with your husband anymore.

There is a slight problem that can prevent you from getting what you came for in this book. You see, there are several concepts that are so simple that you may miss the impact God wants you to have. If it seems way too simple, you have to see it as a red flag for you to take notice and do it. It's like, *of course I need to pick up my feet in order to walk through the door*. Don't miss this because it makes all the difference in surviving your marriage. Remember the parable about the Word falling on gravel and thorns? Show up. Be the good soil.

The other problem is that you have probably read or heard most of the scripture included in this book. The reason that is a problem is that you heard it all before and our minds tend to gloss over what is repeated over and over. You know how you've driven to the grocery store for the thousandth time, then as you pulled into the parking spot, you thought, "Gosh, I don't even remember if I stopped at the stop sign on the way here. I was on autopilot." The same thing can happen here. Be sure to pay conscious attention to what you "already" know.

I don't know why God chose to show me this path of how to change my circumstances and help others to change theirs. But this book has the potential to do just that—change your world. You could actually have peace tonight when your husband gets home. He may not find something to crab at you about. Get a handle on these keys so you can unlock these doors of truth for yourself. Not doing so could hurt you and your chances for living happily ever after. I pray that this book be worn and dog-eared as a symbol of its transformation in your life, your husband, and all those you know and love.

Please, I ask you three things: keep praying, keep close to God, and keep reading this book until you actually see what God wants you to know. You'll know.

What's the Difference?

The way I help Christian women survive their marriage—whether it's through workshops, classes, or one-on-one coaching—is different than what you've tried in the past. Let me explain.

First, I consider myself a communications coach, not a counselor, or a relationship coach. I believe communication is key to any relationship. It's communication that makes or breaks a relationship. My keys do not need your husband to participate at all for you to get relief from his drunken tirades!

I named my company Epiphany Approach because we create a framework that nurtures your innate ability to communicate with God in order to get an epiphany about what you should do, what you should say, how you should say it, and importantly, when to say it to your husband.

Second, as mentioned before, we've read these Bible verses over and over about how we are triumphant in Christ Jesus so many times that I am saddened that so few of us Christian women know how live in Christ in such a way as to be able to transform our men, our marriage, and our planet.

It's not our fault we haven't made the impact on him that we've been going for all these years. God knows all that you have tried. He knows about your bleeding tongue from trying to keep your mouth shut every other day to prevent yourself from saying what you'd probably regret.

I was teaching these keys to county jail inmates who had sentences of incarceration for a few days up to a year. I showed them how to interpret what was going on with the person that was driving them crazy and that lead them to notice how they were they were contributing to their own turmoil. After they continued, daily, working with the keys, their transformation was so complete they were forgetting how bad the situation was weeks earlier. I had to develop an intensity scale so they could see and remember how bad it really was. The intensity scale goes from 1 to 10, 1 is like blissful heaven and a 10 is like fiery abyss. We will use this tool to gauge how well a key worked and how a situation has improved later on.

I was just reminiscing about this phenomenon with Jessica, a past client, who's been married for seventeen years and has two kids in high school now. I met her after a talk I gave at her church. She said, "The other day I was reading an old journal and wow, my life is in such contrast to what it was! My home used to be filled with so much hatred. I was at a ten on the intensity scale most of the time. Now it is much kinder and more loving. Remembering what I went through made me so thankful that I am now living at an intensity of about a three or four most of the time."

When I met Jessica, she was on a mission to figure out how, when her husband returned from rehab, again, she could manage to keep the peace she had in her home. She loved her husband. She wanted to have her marriage persevere through the fiery abyss and come out of it with a testimony of God's ability to heal the brokenness and redeem the love and care they had for each other when they started out. She got her dream come true.

Victory

The keys I present are not my own, but come from God. He told us all about them in the Bible and I get to tell you about how the mystery and the promises opened up for me by applying them to my crappy marriage and my husband's drinking and the tantrums that always followed.

These keys are common and yet profound when used to open doors you thought were locked tight. Since the beginning of time they've been available to you and if you use them, your marriage will transform. You will get less of what you don't want and much more of what you do want.

But first, can you even imagine it? Can you imagine what it's like to not get all twisted up in knots before he walks through the door? Can you imagine being able to know what his real problem is—and fixing it before it escalates? Have you dreamed of having more control and assertiveness? Feel it now—feel the order and peace that contrasts with the turmoil you have now.

"For I know the plans I have for you, declares the Lord. Plans to prosper you and not to harm you, plans to give you a hope and a future. Then you will call upon me and come and pray to me and I will listen to you. You will seek me and find me when you seek me with all your heart. I will be found by you, declares the Lord, and I will bring you back from captivity." (Jeremiah 29:11-14)

These keys are the answer to the questions: Lord, how can I keep living like this? When is he going to hit bottom? There is fear behind those questions. Once we face these fears, answers will be obvious. On one hand, we can't wait for him to hit bottom so we can begin healing and feel the loving intimacy again and, on the other hand, we're terrified of the consequences of what that bottom might bring. Would he lose his job or would we lose the house or will it take someone's death before he quits drinking? Would any of those terrible things even make him stop?

Here's the thing, I've worked with many women trying to survive their husband's drinking and, at some point, you have to face the fear and know that you were born to overcome this. It's time to remove the obstacles between you and a good marriage, obstacles of not knowing how, not understanding, not hearing God—or not being obedient to what He is telling you. That's right.

Sometimes we fear having what we want. The fear of not knowing what it would be like if we didn't have the drama cycle play out in our life every other day. Sometimes we unconsciously fear that even if our dream comes true that it will just set us up for a harder fall.

There's also martyrdom. Right now, you're the Christian wife who bears the cross of living with a ranting alcoholic (even if no one else in the world knows it). Honestly, now, who would you be without this cross to bear?

Be victorious. Know your enemy. Do not use the weapons of this world any longer. Use the Keys of the Kingdom. Nothing but you can stop you. *"No, in all these things we are more than conquerors through him who loved us. For I am convinced that neither death nor life, neither angels nor demons, neither the present nor the future, nor any powers, neither height nor depth, nor anything else in all creation, will be able to separate us from the love of God that is in Christ Jesus our Lord."* (Romans 8:37-39)

CHAPTER 2

Who Am I to Help You?

I owe a lot to the man that would become my husband. He was very smart and got good grades. We did a lot of studying together. I wish I would have had the gumption to consider it a potential future problem when my boyfriend would often take a Jumbo (40oz beer) up to the library to study. But he was so handsome, had such a great sense of humor, and so sexy! His parents just loved me right from the start and I loved them. I felt like I belonged. This was the man I was going to spend the rest of my life with.

I was still at school, and we were talking about marriage. Looking at rings. We found one and picked it up from the store one day. And that was it. We were getting married. That day we brought the ring home was the day I really felt married to him. We talked about where we wanted to live, how many children we wanted, and that "divorce was not an option." Little did I know that those words actually gave him license to be awful and confident so he could walk all over me.

We married in October of 1988 and 7 months later I was pregnant. He wanted to abort the child and spent about a week trying to convince me we couldn't afford, and were not ready for a child. Somehow, I gained composure and just simply called up his parents and told them. They were ecstatic and for the first time I felt excited, too! The idea grew on him and soon he was excited too.

Up until I got pregnant, we would party all the time, doing cocaine often. When he was on cocaine he was so "normal." Not angry, but gentle, kind and happy-go-lucky. It was truly amazing. Night and Day. Like Dr. Jekyll and Mr. Hyde because when he would come down from the high, look out! I once had to call his brother to come to the house because he was at the bedroom door with a knife. That day, I resolved never to do coke again.

The moment I knew I was pregnant, partying was over. That's when things really began to come into focus. Wow! He was really screwed up. And now I was pregnant. I did nothing. After all, I loved him and, "Divorce was not an option." Our son was born in 1990, and his daddy really stepped into the role. He adores his son!

About two and half years later, on December 5th, 1992, I realized I was pregnant again. That same afternoon he got a great big letter in the mail. He was being sued for paternity. His daughter was born on our son's due date. He had been having an affair during our whole engagement. No wonder he would go into jealous rages. He was doing the thing he was afraid I would do to him.

Well, now I was pregnant with number two. How could I leave now, besides, "Divorce was not an option." I loved my husband. There was such a great person inside that ball of anger. I would experience it about once every three or four days. He was a closet drinker. So, he would get hammered, get angered, rage, and pass out. The next day he would be remorseful and nice, loving. Then a day or two later he would be angry all over again until he would finally drink and the cycle started all over again.

I Got Help

After I stopped working outside the home, my girlfriend asked me to go to Ladies Bible Study with her at Walloon Lake Church. I immersed myself in God's word.

One night at my desk doing the study in the Gospel of John, His word gently cuddled my heart and I just gave it up. I gave myself to him. I said, "Okay God, if you will have me, I trust you. Please live in me." And that was it. One of the best decisions I have ever made. I don't think I would be alive today if I did not have Jesus to lean on, to talk to, to guide me.

Things didn't really get better, actually, they got worse. The closer I got to Jesus the more alienated my husband felt. He often called me a holy roller, Bible thumper, and so on. Rest assured; I was not perfect by any means. I was usually thinking about myself, and I was that nagging wife the Bible talks about. I was so hard to live with.

> *"The steady dripping of rain and the nagging of a wife are one and the same."*
> –Proverbs 27:15

However, my life as a mother and friend flourished. I began to see God in everything in my world. He soon gave us a home right on Lake Charlevoix. What an idyllic world to raise my children. We swam in the summer, boated, fished, ice fished in the winter, snowmobiled, had amazing sunrises and sunsets, and every day was beautiful, even the cloudy ones.

He was drinking more often. I could never tell if he was just hungry or drunk. He was a tyrant either way. Screaming at me nightly for something or other. I couldn't do anything right or when he expected it. I was a basket case just before he came home from work. I didn't realize how crazy I was until one day a friend happened to be over when he pulled in the driveway. I jumped up and started picking everything up and straightening the curtains to make the house look like a hotel room with everything in its place. She just sat there and watched me—wide eyed with surprise.

He would slam his heels on the floor as he walked around the house inspecting things. Not in front of my friend of course. This was just for my benefit.

Once a week, six of us ladies would get together to do the Bible study while the children played together. We meticulously studied God's word, prayed for each other, our families, our churches, our community, and things going on in the world. We became so close, and so close to God. We would enjoy experiencing God in each other's lives. Such an amazing time. We still get together once a year for a weekend.

One day, my friend came to my home to help me see that things were not good. My friends were afraid for my life. You see, my husband would often pretend to shoot me. Pretend to shoot me with a bow and arrow, or act like he was holding a pistol to my head and say, "Pow...Pow, pow!" My friends and I fasted several times, prayed God's word and blessings over us. I was transforming, but he was getting worse. So much so, that the girls believed I needed to get outside help.

I made a few phone calls and ended up in a twelve-step group for overcoming codependency. I was so devoted to saving my marriage that I drove an hour and ten minutes every week for almost two years. I got a healthy mind. God gave me skills to deal with my husband's anger flare-ups. He blessed me and blessed me. God coordinated it all.

I changed. God changed me from within. I could experience my husband's rage without getting sucked into it by screaming back or trying to reason through the anger. I was not numb to it, however. I felt it and understood it, and loved my husband anyway. I loved him even though he was awful to me at times.

I worked so hard to stay married, but God did not save our marriage. As I look back on it, I see now that He had a greater purpose for everything I went through. I had to walk through it so I could help you, but He wanted me to be able to help you for a lifetime and not just for a night or two in a Victorian home with gardens and a beautiful view like I had dreamed about. He wanted you to experience His promises every day forever. I kept my nose in God's word and took classes and went to seminars to heal, to know God, to change me.

Soon after God opened doors for me to teach these stress relieving skills to inmates in county jails in Northern Michigan and teach community education courses at the University Center in Gaylord. It provided a fantastic income and I learned so much about running my own business, but mostly it was the shift that I helped so many people experience. They used their skills to turn around a bad situations. It was the lightbulb that went on in their head when they realized how different their situation was now that they looked at it differently. They could change— that their situations could improve by a shift in their focus.

It was in teaching my stress relieving classes that I began attracting Christian wives whose marriages were filled with turmoil. And I knew, I just knew God had me experience all that so I could help you.

I used to *wonder* if staying in my marriage was the right decision for our children. They were exposed to so much anger for so long. My daughter phoned the other day to tell me how her boss gave her a $200 bonus for handling an irate client with grace. He was very impressed. I was very blessed to have an answer to my *wonder*ing! You will be able to handle your husband with the Grace of God, like Jesus would, and be blessed. You have God's support. You have my support.

Want to be prayed for daily? Reach out to me so I can add you to my daily prayer at: www.epiphanyapproach. com/prayer.

Truth

I believe, totally, in the information contained in this book. I know that it is 100% truth just as I know the

Law of Gravity is real. You, however, may not believe it is 100% truth. You may, after completing your read, feel it is something less than pure truth. That is okay because even if you believe that it is only sometimes true, it will sometimes make your relationship with your husband better. Most importantly, I ask you to put this information to the test. Be curious, be thorough. Put into practice just what works for you and leave the rest behind. In other words, if it makes sense to you, then use that part.

And…

I promise there will be things in this book that will rub you the wrong way. In fact, you may get so agitated you may be tempted to throw the book against the wall. There are two ways to handle it. One is to not read another word and go on with your life as is. The other is to persevere and let it go. Don't give that part any attention and move on to the next chapter, and the next chapter after that, until the problem gets better.

I love that you are reading this book to improve your relationship with your husband. I pray that the way you handle yourself and others will be transformed into the likeness of Christ Jesus.

> *"Though we walk in the flesh, we are not waging war according to the flesh."*
> –2 Corinthians 10:4

If you are like I was, you are probably waging war in the flesh way more often than not. The following prayer gets us into a key position:

Father God,

I bind my will to your will, my reality to your truth. I bind my life to the life, death, and resurrection of Jesus and to His saving blood. I also bind my self-talk and my mind to the mind of Christ. I LOOSE, CRUSH, SMASH, DESTROY, TEAR DOWN AND SHATTER THE STRONGHOLDS protecting my wrong attitudes, wrong beliefs and behaviors, wrong desires, and wrong habits and ideas. I loose and shatter all influences of this wrong thinking as well as all generational sin in my life. In the precious name of Jesus Christ, AMEN.

I love You, God. I love You and am so thankful for all Your blessings.

Yours Always,

[Your Name]

I am here for you, and of course you know God is here for you in your heart. But wouldn't it be amazing to actually see God, to see Him orchestrating all this turmoil for your and your husband's benefit? And wouldn't it be nice to have a helping hand, someone who could listen to your specific problem and remind you of your options?

CHAPTER 3

What You'll Get

This is what you've been praying for. When the angry alcoholic side of your husband shows up again, you'll need these skills if you're going to see this marriage through fifty more years. I will lay out the steps, taken directly from God's Word, that have helped my clients communicate with their husbands in a brand-new way. They don't get sucked into their husband's arguments any more, they can make him stop yelling, reduce the intensity and frequency of his rants. And they know exactly what his real problem is! Plus, they know exactly what God is trying to tell them, immediately.

Here is how I am going to help you:

Chapter 4: First Key—Start with God, start with Jesus. When your husband comes home all hopped up and his face is two inches from yours yelling about a bunch of nothing, as usual, you're going to call on Jesus. Just watch what happens next!

Chapter 5: Second Key—Get the wind in your sails. Start by getting Jesus to fill every cell in your body, to expel all the bad out and suck all the goodness of the Holy Spirit in. This will transform you, your husband, and the whole room.

Chapter 6: Third Key—Learn the importance of the word. Your words are so powerful. Learn about what God thinks about the words you and your husband speak. What those words actually mean and how they relate to his drinking problem. This knowledge will give you power to deal with him and your reaction to how he speaks to you.

Chapter 7: Fourth Key—Learn the power of non-verbal communication. Know what it really means when he won't hug you back or when he gives you the silent treatment or calls you names or is always leaving whiskers in the sink. You will know how to speak his silent language.

Chapter 8: Fifth Key—Discover the Epiphany Approach. Learn how to know what he is really thinking, what's really motivating him and exactly what you can do about it. You'll learn what God is trying to tell you. I know it sounds unbelievable, but Jesus used parables all the time—2,000 years ago and today. Let me show you how it can help transform your marriage.

Chapter 9: Sixth Key—Unlock the most difficult door. Grab hold of the key that will release your fear and get you unstuck. I'll be there for you every step of the way. Let's get started.

Chapter 10: Seventh Key—Sending forth. I will wrap the whole book up in my prayer for you.

CHAPTER 4

Jesus, Take the Wheel

The most important key to surviving your husband's drunken tirades is calling on Jesus by name to help you. Jesus is literally the key to heaven because the moment you call on His name you have an unseen mountain-moving power working to help you!

Protection

> *"The Lord will fight for you,*
> *and you have only to be silent."*
> –Exodus 14:14

God does not ask you to do His fighting for Him. The battle with your husband is not your battle, even though when he is being nasty to you in that moment it seems crushing. When his voice raises, when he is trying to make you feel small, take notice. You have a choice. Do all the things you usually do, slam doors, stomp around, cry, walk/run away, but while you are doing those things, be silent outwardly. Inside, have a conversation with God. Remind Him this is His battle, not yours. Connect with God inside of you. He is with you in everything you do. When you are in the bathroom, in the car, while you're eating and sleeping, and even right now in this very moment. When you get the feeling of hopelessness, go in. Recognize HIS presence—from there His peace emanates. Glean from the following examples and recognize how the Lord has been there for you, too, during similar experiences.

Praise Jesus Story

"As long as Moses held up his hands,
the Israelites were winning,
but whenever he lowered his hands,
the Amalekites were winning."
–Exodus 17:11

My daughter and I were in her room. She had just done something so cute. She looked so beautiful and I was filled with gratitude for having her in my life. She is such a joy! At this same time, my furious husband began stomping up the stairs saying, "HEY! I…" meanwhile I was completely filled with "happy" and raising my hands above my head saying, "Praise the Lord for my Punkin'!" I met my husband at the top of the stairs. Our eyes locked, mine with a smile from deep in my soul and his with pure fury. In a split moment, he looked at me with total bewilderment, completely forgetting what he was going to yell at me about! I was delighted in the Lord, again, and gave my husband smiles, hugs, and kisses! He never even knew what hit him! He was dumfounded and enjoyed the surprise, too. Give it a try. Be so joyous and grateful that it extinguishes ill will.

Jesus Rescues: Refrigerator Story

*"…Call upon me in the day of trouble; I will
deliver you, and you will honor me."*
–Psalm 50:15

One time we were in the kitchen getting ready for dinner. My husband was drunk, screaming at me in front of the kids. He got right in my face, "Who have you been effing, huh? Who? I want to know! I know you are screwing me over!" I opened the refrigerator door to put it between us. I was paralyzed, hanging on to the door handle with all my might. I closed my eyes and inside myself, called slowly, "Jesus…. Jesus…. Jesus, please give me something to say to make him stop."

I had been eating at the table with the kids for at least ten minutes before I realized that he wasn't attacking me anymore. He had gone up to bed. Jesus didn't give me anything to say. He rescued me instead.

Kiss My God's Butt Story

"The seventy-two returned with joy and said, 'LORD, even the demons submit to us in your name.'"
–Luke 10:17

One evening my husband was drunk and had been nasty for quite a while. I was aggravated when I found that he put the children in our bed to sleep for the night, so I laid down in my son's bed instead. As I gazed at the ceiling I praised the Lord for a little bit, and then my husband came in all crabby and ranting about something as I continued to pray to the Lord asking Him to, "Fill up the room, fill up this whole house with the love of Jesus." At that moment, he stopped, backed out of the room, and slammed the door as he went. When he got to the bottom of the stairs, he yelled up the stairs to me in anger, "Your God can *kiss* my god's butt!" My eyes were bulging. I had not even opened my mouth. He had no idea what I was thinking—praying. With a sad heart, I immediately prayed, "Lord, forgive him for he does not know what he just did."

Wow! God totally answered that prayer. Can you imagine? That prayer was like a campfire that started inside of me and immediately filled that bedroom with the essence of Jesus that literally pushed him out of the room and away from me.

> *"And I will do whatever you ask in my name, so that the Father may be glorified in the Son. You may ask me for anything in my name, and I will do it. If you love me, keep my commands."*
> —John 14:13-15

How About You?

Jesus actually commands you to ask Him to do stuff for you. In light of your husband being out of control, it is on you to ask Jesus to get involved. It's like the moment you go in and ask for His help, He puts you in a fireproof safe and He performs miracles! John 10:9 says, *"I am the gate; whoever enters through me will be saved. He will come in and go out, and find pasture."* Go in to be with Jesus. Look out to see His mighty work.

Journal your past experiences of Him fighting for you, rescuing you, protecting you even if you didn't actually ask him for help. Expect to be able to journal new big WOW experiences of Christ's intervention during your husband's drunken tirades.

Tip the Scale:

Record the date, time, place and what happened after you called on the name of Jesus to help you.

CHAPTER 5

Just Breathe

"I will put breath in you, and you will come to life. Then you will know that I am the Lord."
–Ezekiel 37:6b

Have you ever tried to make a chocolate cake without chocolate or cook chicken without a heat source? It just can't be done. You need just enough of all the right ingredients to obtain the best results. Same is true about you in whatever you are trying to accomplish. Your body needs 3 essential ingredients in order to function properly, let alone respond to your irate husband.

You must have food within about forty days or your organs begin to have irreparable damage. You must have water within three to five days or who knows what kind of damage will be done. Now air, air is another thing entirely. It is your most essential ingredient. Breathing is the very first thing you do when you enter into this world and it is the last thing you will do when your life here is finished. Breathing gives you life.

Breathing. Sounds too simple to be the miracle key that can transform everything about your relationship, but it is. It is so simple that you might miss just how powerful this key is. It's like gravity. You can struggle to get the ketchup out of the bottle by slamming it on the table, pounding it with the back of your hand, swirling a knife in it, or you can just simply store it upside down and let gravity do the work for you.

It is the same way with air. When you and your husband are arguing, or he is yelling at you, you aren't breathing. At most, you might take a shallow breath. One time I was on the phone with my husband and all of a sudden, I noticed that I wasn't breathing. I had simply stopped taking in air. It was like I was protecting myself with a wall of "Nothing is going in and nothing is going out." Not breathing can be the cause of explosions in your relationship because all that pent-up energy pro-duces a boiling point.

The thing is, the conversation I was having with my

husband was no big deal. My "not breathing" was not caused by the content of our conversation.

I simply decided to breathe the moment I realized I wasn't, and the conversation changed. I felt better. He felt better, and by the end of the call, we were joking around and hung up the phone with smiles on our faces.

"But it is the spirit in a man, the breath of the Almighty, that gives him understanding."
–Job 32:8

This non-breathing thing that you do during stressful times or when you're with stressful people, or when you are thinking about your stress, keeps you solidly entrenched in your stress. When you are crying, and upset you are contracted. Your body naturally caves in. Every time I've found my face buried deeply in my hands I know I am not breathing!

Here is the other reason to breathe. The dictionary captured it perfectly. Breathe: 1b. to become perceptible. The old adage "take a breather" is real because it gives us a new perspective. If you want all the brainpower to tackle the problem in front of you, you need to get air in so all those neurotransmitters can fire off.

"This is what God the Lord says—He who created the heavens and stretched them out, who

spread out the earth and all that comes out of it,
who gives breath to its people, and life to those
who walk on it: 'I, the Lord, have called you in
righteousness; I will take hold of your hand.'"
–Isaiah 42:5-6a

Getting air inside you will not only give you knowledge to transform how you handle your husband, but it will be like God reaching down to give you a hand. According to David S. Dyer, if you are experiencing overall weakness, poor digestion, muscle pain or aches, fatigue, dizziness, depression, circulation problems, memory loss, irritability, irrational behavior, acid stomach, or bronchial problems, it may be because of an oxygen deficiency. When the immune system doesn't get the air it needs, you are more susceptible to bacterial, viral, or parasitic infections, as well as colds and the flu. It is known that cancers and infectious diseases cannot live in an oxygen rich environment. Oxygen disintegrates and destroys toxins and any useless substances. Give your body it's most essential ingredient and it will be better able to handle whatever it is exposed to, especially your husband's drunken tirades.

Tip the Scale: Air Exercise

First, think about the last time your husband went on a rant. On the intensity scale of 1 being heaven and 10 being fiery abyss, what is your number?

Two points of caution: 1) Do this at your own risk, you know your situation, I do not. 2) it is important that this process be balanced. Get as much air as you can out and as much as you can in. If it is done lopsided, you may experience dizziness.

It is my strongest recommendation that you get air into your body any way you can under any stressful situation. However, the following method has proven effective. First, touch the tip of your tongue to the back of your teeth and slide it back to the bumpy ridge of between your teeth and the roof of your mouth. Keep it there for the whole process. This has something to do with your energy and how it travels in your body. Think of it as electricity. There is a negative and positive polarity in your body and by placing your tongue in this position it completes the current. It keeps the energy circulating in the body instead of allowing it to escape or dissipate.

Next, gear up your mind and choose what you are going to say to yourself such as, "Out with the bad, in with the good." Or, you may choose to be more visual by "seeing'" in your mind's eye every molecule leaving your body through your nose. Your mission is to expel every bit of breath from your body and take as much air in as you possibly can. Exhale by squeezing all the air out of your chest and gut by contracting your body, head down, shoulders forward, and chest and gut squeezed tightly while saying in your mind, "Out with the bad, out with the bad." Then I squeeze a little more out. Hold for a second. Then breathe in. Through the nose expanding your chest and tummy as you say to yourself, "In with the good. In with the good. God get in here." Keep sucking in air through your nose until you're almost about to hold your breath and then give it one more inhale effort, hold for a second and then let it all out through your nose. Now do two more sets for a total of three. I always have a wide smile on my face when I'm done. It makes me feel great! I suppose it could be because of how ridiculous I look, alone, but it works!

Now if you just did that exercise you feel lighter, better. Now as you think of that last time he went on a rant, what is your new number on the intensity scale? I know it is less intense now.

If you want to help yourself heal and bring the hand of God into your situation, breathe. Go behind closed doors if you have to, your car, the bathroom, outside, in an empty hall. Do whatever you have to. Do it right in front of someone incognito without them knowing.

"Draw near to God and
He will draw near to you..."
–James 4:8

Are you sleeping at night? If you are tossing and turning with your mind going a hundred miles an hour along the road to misery and you just can't shut it down... breathe! Get God's lifeforce deep into your soul. My clients report amazing results with just one set of three breaths. They feel better, not as constipated, and they find their husbands are being less intense, conversations happen more, and arguments happen less.

CHAPTER 6

Words are Powerful

"For this is the message that
you have heard from the beginning,
that we should love one another."
−1 John 3:11

Remember the scene from *Pretty Woman* where Vivian is describing how she ended up a prostitute? She makes a profound statement that you and I can relate to. She says, "People put you down enough, you start to believe it."

It is heart-wrenching when your husband calls you a slut or a slug, or says that you were late or that it was not done right or that you're an idiot, on and on it goes. Those words begin to affect how you think about yourself. Nothing you don't already know, but there is a science to it.

Hidden Messages

Masaru Emoto, is the author of the *Hidden Messages in Water* and a photographer of ice crystals. He exposed water to beautiful music, gorgeous pictures, or words like love and wisdom, thank you, and relax, and crystals formed in spectacular shapes. When he exposed the water to pictures, words, and music that were negative like "I hate you," or pictures of garbage dumps, the crystals were either malformed or the water did not form a crystal at all. In another experiment, when water samples were taken from this particular lake, the ice crystals didn't form. That same lake was prayed over and those samples taken after the prayer formed beautiful, intricate fronds.

The point is that you and your husband and everyone else on this planet consist of about 70% water. If water has a hard time forming crystals if exposed to negativity—negative words, negative looks, harsh tones, negative thoughts, then you will also have a hard time functioning at your best potential.

You could say that there is a scientific reason why Christ commands us to love.

In the Beginning

*"Seeing a fig tree by the road, He went up to
it but found nothing on it except leaves. Then
He said to it, 'May you never bear fruit again!'
Immediately the tree withered."*
–Matthew 21:19

Your husband uses words to put you down. Those words have had a lot of power over you. You have just as much power. Let's see what God has to say about you because this darkness that you are in has a light at the end of the tunnel.

So many have come before you who, like you, have walked in darkness. Oprah Winfrey lived in poverty as a little girl. She is now one of the richest women in the world. Abraham Lincoln lost several elections before becoming president. We were so close to losing the Revolutionary War, but George Washington crossed the Potomac River and was victorious. Abram and Sara were barren without children for a hundred years, then they conceived. Garth Brooks wrote a song "Thank God for Unanswered Prayers" and in the video he shows how he, later in life, runs into a girl who he wanted to marry, but he is so grateful for the woman he has now. My parents divorced when I was eight years old. It devastated me, but I am so grateful for what I experienced because it prepared me for what I do today. I am so grateful for that tragedy. Jesus hung on a cross and is now seated at the right hand of the Father.

You are at the precipice just by reading this book. You have read Genesis. Let's take a closer look.

> *"Then God said, 'Let us make man in our image,
> in our likeness, and let them rule over the fish of
> the sea and the birds of the air, over the livestock,
> over all the earth, and over all the creatures that
> move along the ground.' So God created man in
> His own image, in the image of God He created
> him; male and female He created them."*
> –Genesis 1:26-27

Do you suppose that if God really did make you in His image, in His likeness, that you might do some things like He does them?

Well, what did God do? Let's go back to His very first words to us in Genesis 1:1: "God created." It seems to reason that if you were, in fact, created in God's image that you would do what He did. We create. Look around you right now. There is not a single thing you can lay your eyes on that was not created, either by us or God. Not one thing.

You are in that same place God was when he created everything. Genesis 1:2, "Now the earth was formless and empty, darkness was over the surface of the deep and the Spirit of God was hovering over the waters." This could be you now. We can infer that as God hovered over the earth that was formless and empty and dark that He was contemplating what He wanted. He was making decisions and processing what He would do first, then second, and so on.

You do this all the time. You have a thought or a desire, "I'm hungry." You hover over the refrigerator, consider all your options, decide what you want, then go about taking the steps necessary to getting it into your mouth. It began from within. It begins with a concept. All things are created, first, in the mind.

So how, exactly, did God create? Seven times he tells us.

Genesis 1:3 *And God said*, let there be light

Genesis 1:6 *And God said*, expanse separates

Genesis 1:9 *And God said*, dry land appear

Genesis 1:11 *Then God said*, vegetation

Genesis 1:14 *And God said*, sun and moon

Genesis 1:20 *And God said*, sea and sky creatures

Genesis 1:24 *And God said*, animals, and man the sixth day

From the very beginning God was teaching us that he "said" things into existence. He began his communication with us by telling us the most important thing he wanted us to learn about Him and ultimately about ourselves.

Genesis 1 is similar to our first-grade textbook in school. "A" is for apple and we hear it, and we see it, and we feel it until we get it. The Bible refers to creation over 300 times. It's like God says, "I hovered, I said, and it was so and I saw it was good and I call it what it is." He did this seven times just to be sure you got it.

And we do the same thing, right? The following is a typical conversation, "Sara, did you hear what happened to Frank? Didn't I tell you he was heading for a fall? I told him this was going to happen! I told him every day! I had nightmares about it. I worried about it all the time. I could see it happening. I am devastated about it, but it comes as no surprise."

You Do Some Things Like God Does

This is so relevant to what you have in your life right now. There are so many things you say that lead you to having exactly what you say. "I'm never going to get that job. It's going to rain on the parade. I'm sure of it. I just know it is going to work out okay." How many times have you said things like that and that is what actually happened?

This is the beginning of creating a new paradigm in your marriage. Let's start by looking around at what is good in your world right now. That's what God did. Lift your eyes from this page and gaze around you. What do you see that is good? How are you feeling right now?

Hopeful? Find something in your presence that is good. This is the whole reason you are reading this book.

Like Masaru Emoto discovered, what you think about and focus on, affects your insides. I am not implying that if you say "cup of coffee," it will appear. What I am saying is that if you say over and over that "he is a big jerk." I'll bet he oftentimes shows up being a big jerk! The same goes for him. He says over and over, "You're a nag." Sure enough, you show up being a nag.

Words, Over Time, are Literal

"I just don't have a grip." I used to say that all the time. I didn't really realize that I said it until one day I was backing up my jeep. It was winter so I had engaged four-wheel drive. It was a tight spot so I had to really crank the steering wheel as I applied the gas, the steering wheel kicked back hard and fast and before I knew what happened, the fingers on my right hand were THROBBING in pain. A week goes by. Swelling goes down, but I have definitely screwed up my middle finger's knuckle. I could still use my hand, but I couldn't really get a good grip on all kinds of things. I was carrying groceries in and I thought to myself "I just don't have a grip!" IT HIT ME LIKE A TON OF BRICKS (i.e., epiphany). I SAY THAT TO MYSELF ALL THE TIME! When that old, not good for me statement floats into my consciousness, I now have a choice. I can keep saying in my head what I don't want, or I can say, "I do actually have a grip." Hunting around on the inside of me until I find a few things I do have a grip on really helps me. It changes me and my circumstances. "Hey," I say to myself, "I have a grip on the laundry." "I have a grip on my classroom." "I have a grip on what I am teaching." The result is that I begin to notice more things I have a grip on and the things I do not have a good grip on begin to leave my experience. God is so good!

What You Say Every Day

Our quips are so innocent at first. You start out idly saying something. It has a little bit of truth to it and it rolls right off the tongue and before you know it, you've said it a few times a week and then something miraculous happens. The thing you said begins to show up. You are so smart! You proudly proclaim your catchy phrase and watch your listeners agree with you so that they, too, can begin to look for ways in which the world lines up with your catchy phrase.

You have heard these examples your whole life. The grass is always greener on the other side. I'm behind the eight ball. It's hard. The economy is bad. It won't last forever. I knew he was going to leave me. I knew she was going to get caught. I knew they were going to lay me off. I knew it was too good to be true.

Take a moment and consider. What quip do you say all the time? How is that statement showing up in your reality? Think of that thing that your husband says all the time. Is it showing up in his life, too?

I used to get speeding tickets all the time. I used the same process that God did to create the world. The whole time I was speeding I would focus my eyes way down the road as far as I could see because I wanted to see the police car well in advance. I was looking to get caught, wasn't I? I kept imagining the police care over each hill or around each corner. I was picturing it in my mind while I was expecting to see it. I was also working up the story I would give the policeman when I got pulled over. Do you see the creative process happening here? I really don't get speeding tickets anymore because I have stopped thinking that way, and of course I've slowed down a bit.

Now the question to ask is, how do I change this around knowing that both you and your husband are speaking exactly what you are spending your time worrying about, thinking about, and talking about all the time? Let's tip the intensity scale together.

Tip the Scale: Focus on the Good

My clients stopped focusing on what they did not want and instead began spending time on what they wanted and they got more of the good stuff. Do you want more of the good stuff of your marriage? Focus in on that. Journal your memories of the good times. Describe them in detail. Who was there, what were you wearing, what was the weather like, what were the tones of voice used, what were you feeling, what was said and how was it said, what was the order of how things happened, what were you eating, what were you smelling, and what did you know about it? Again, spending time on good brings you more good.

> *"And the second is this, 'You shall love your neighbor as yourself.' There is no other commandment greater than these."*
> –Mark 12:31

Tip the Scale: I Love You

Get in front of a mirror and look at yourself. Look right into your eyes and say "I love you," for at least the next sixty seconds. Do two minutes tomorrow and the next day do an additional minute. Keep going until you get to five minutes. Set a timer.

Tip the Scale: Focus

You are always in a state of creation. Think about, pray about, write about, take pictures of, draw about, listen to, look at, and notice what you love, who you love, when you love, where you love, and why you love.

What excites you, makes you happy, makes you feel good, calm, and content? Spend fifteen consecutive minutes every day focusing on these things. Use your watch or clock with a minute hand.

Notice how you begin to notice additional things you love throughout your day. Add them to your list. Be delighted with what begins to show up in your life. Notice that what you love starts showing up more often. Note how long you were able to be in that gratefulness state before you thought of something negative or off focus. Those negative thoughts are what I call little buggers. You know, that annoying voice that is always keeping you small, reminding you of how you are not good enough. It's your little bugger that keeps you stuck.

Notice the little bugger in your head that tries to drag your thoughts toward the yucky stuff. Just notice the contrast. Be delighted with yourself that you noticed. Start now, focusing on what you love, and do it every day for fifteen minutes. This should be pleasurable. Don't do it if it is not. Don't feel guilty about not doing it, remember you'll just be feeding your little bugger and that part of your life you desire less of.

Here is the truth of the matter, you are not in control of your spouse, your kids, your job, your family, the people you work with, your boss, the economy, the weather, the guy that cut you off on the freeway, your neighbor, or your friend. Some of you may like to think you have control and some of you may manipulate every aspect of someone's life, but in the end, if they have a brain, you don't actually have complete control of them. If you are fortunate enough to have them do what you have manipulated them to do, you may have noticed that deep down it didn't turn out as well as it would have if they would have done it of their own accord. Do you know what I mean? The real deal is that the ONLY thing you have control over is how LONG you spend with an accusation or judgment.

If you want more love, if you want more of what Jesus has to offer, if you would like to love like Jesus does—even love your angry alcoholic—get in front of the mirror and love yourself. You will have exponentially more love to give. It is just like the flight attendant says, "Put the oxygen mask to your mouth first so you can help others around you." Pure truth.

The more you practice this, the less crap will come your way sooner than later. It's like feeding or not feeding a stray cat. Have you ever fed a stray cat? For a while it is okay and then you start noticing a lot of chaos in your back yard with more cats showing up to be fed. After you have had enough, you stop feeding the stray cats. But what happens? They start coming around at all times of the night and day meowing and meowing at your doors and windows pouring on the pressure for you to feed them. Your little buggers are like that. But if you stick to your guns by not feeding them, they begin to come around a little less often, and a week or so goes by and you only see them a couple of times and before you know it, they don't come around anymore because they weren't getting fed. Same goes for that little bugger in your head.

It's Hard!

How about the phrase, "It's hard"? Do you hear the people you are around use that phrase? Do you say that phrase? It's hard to find a job in this economy. It's hard to pay the prices at the gas pump. It's hard to stay sober. It's hard to be nice to him. It's hard work to keep a marriage together. It's hard to keep up with the Joneses. It's hard to balance home and work. It's hard to keep the house clean. It's hard for me to find the time to exercise.

Add your "it's hard" phrase that you say all the time to that list. Go ahead. Say it out loud. Make that be the last time you say it out loud. The thought may or may not float back into your consciousness in the future. But that should be the last time it goes airborne!

Now you know how powerful our words are. I showed you how science proves the power of your words, and that God wanted to make sure you knew how you were made in His image and that the very first thing He taught us in the Bible was that words create. Keep tipping the scale toward heaven on earth and sooner than later you'll get more of heaven than hell.

It is time to reveal to you the silent languages that are spoken loud and clear in your home without using words. You use these languages to love and hate and manipulate. When you don't know what they are, they wreak havoc on your homelife. After you become aware of them, they won't be able to undermine your sanity anymore.

CHAPTER 7

Seven Silent Languages

*"How is it then that each of us hears them
in his own native language?"*
–Acts 2:8

My client, Susan, confided in me that every time she walked into a room where her husband, Frank, had been he left something behind. He left whatever he was doing behind and she felt compelled to either ask him to pick it up or to do it herself. It just seemed easier sometimes. She complained, "I feel so unappreciated. I almost never hear a thank you. My husband never wants to spend time with me. It is driving me crazy! He is always complaining that I should just know how much he appreciates me. I am always sure to have everything looking good: the house, his clothes, my appearance. He walked in with a bouquet of flowers for me the other day. Flowers we couldn't afford. I wish he would just help around here."

It is important to know that your husband is speaking a silent language and I want you to know what it is so that you can survive his drunken tirades. There are seven silent languages. I call them silent because for the most part it is a language without words.

If your husband speaks a different silent language than you, then there is no wonder you both are miserable. If you can decipher and understand his dominant silent language, a lot of conflict can be avoided. I trust you will find the answer here to transform what is not working.

It is important to know that nagging is a telltale sign of frustration related to not being spoken to in your silent language. Which one of you is the nag in your relationship. Nag, nag, nag. It's so frustrating! It is as though you are speaking English and your husband is speaking German. There is no rapport, no connection. The relationship becomes very effortful over time. This is not the only cause of nagging, of course, but it is a big one, and if you understand what's going on, you are ahead of the game.

I formed the basis of these seven silent languages from a book called *The Five Love Languages* by Gary Chapman. I read it back in 1995 when I was raising my children and struggling with my marriage. It really made a big impact in my world because I understood the people around me much better. That information then blossomed into a much deeper understanding as I discovered the intricacies of how these silent languages are used not only to love one another, but also to be mean and manipulative to one another.

The seven silent languages are: *The Doer, The Gifter, The Hugger, The Knower, The Looker, The Spotlighter,* and *The Worder.* I have organized them in alphabetical order to help you remember all seven while you try to figure out the dominant silent language you and for him. This will help you communicate with him at a deeper, more effective level. Knowing the seven silent languages puts you at a great advantage in creating a better relationship. You will have greater rapport, camaraderie, respect, and connection with him.

Everyone speaks all seven silent languages. However, there will be one language you rely on, dominantly, and you speak it very fluently, all the time. In other words, it's your most natural language. If you speak a foreign language, probably the language you grew up with is your most dominant. The same is true for your dominant silent language. You naturally speak your native tongue. You don't have to work at it at all.

Remember you use these silent languages to show dislike as well as love. When you are speaking your silent language in a loving manner, you feel good on the inside. When someone else speaks our silent language in a loving way to us, you feel really good. For example, when your friend comes to visit and you both speak English, you both feel rapport with one another and you enjoy the visit. If your friend came to visit and refused to speak your language, it would be so effortful and time-consuming. You both would feel unheard, misunderstood, and frustrated.

Courtship

Have you ever wondered why your romantic relationship with your husband-to-be started out so fantastic and then some time later things seemed to sour and not be quite as wonderful? The reason it starts out so wonderful is because, in the beginning, you are speaking all seven silent languages all the time.

Remember what you were doing in the beginning. You both were thinking ahead and doing things for each other. You were thinking about each other all the time, either spiritually or silently sending happy thoughts. You were both more affectionate, making sure things looked good, spending time with each other, and bringing thoughtful gifts, and noticing and telling each other how wonderful they are. Then, after some time, both partners resort to their comfortable, natural, low-effort, dominant languages. If your silent languages match up, you probably are not interested in this book. If your silent languages do not match up, things have soured because each of you feel empty or disrespected as your silent languages are not spoken. You begin to feel like he is from a foreign country and you can't understand him and he cannot understand you.

Let's Get Ready

There are two ways your silent language depletes you and him. One way occurs when he hardly ever "speaks" your dominant silent language. The other way is when you speak your silent language to him and he doesn't "hear it" or receive it. There are many examples found in the following pages.

I am going to take you through many scenarios of how these silent languages play out in our lives, and from those examples, I will build bridges from your experiences to a place of wisdom, understanding, and love. At the end of this chapter there is a link to a helpful tool to help you know for sure what your husband's dominant silent language is. You will be able to respond to what is really going on in your relationship with your husband. You will have the keys to really unlock your love for one another, at least, and to be able to communicate with him with grace and understanding.

Remember you speak all seven silent languages. We all do things, give things, hug, know things, care about what things look like, want to be noticed, and say nice things. This enables us to understand most other people if we really try. However, we will always resort to our dominant language because they are effortless. Dominance can be easily determined by how often or how intensely one resorts to a particular language.

Be curious; discover. I'll show you Jesus and how He used these silent languages to heal people. You will use them to heal your relationships.

The Doer

> *"He Himself [Jesus] bore our sins in his body*
> *on the tree, so that we might die to sins*
> *and live for righteousness; by His wounds*
> *you have been healed."*
> —1 Peter 2:24

Jesus as the Doer hung on the cross in payment for our sins. He did that!

Jesus did that for us. He is the ultimate Doer!

The Doer and Love

The Doer is someone, who, when they want to say, "I love you" will do something for you. He will do the laundry. He will iron the shirt. He'll do the dishes, make the bed. He will clean out the garage. He will fix something for you. He will notice that the light bulb needs to be changed and he will change it for you. When the Doer is doing something for someone, he is saying he loves her a lot. When he is serving, he feels love on the inside. It makes him feel so good. Basically, a Doer will know what needs to be done.

If someone in the Doer's world does something for him, like all those examples I just listed, the Doer feels good on the inside, too. It just pumps him up. He is so appreciative when he comes home from work and the garbage is taken out and the kitchen is clean. It makes him feel good on the inside because his dominant silent language has been spoken. It's as if he speaks French and the person who cleaned was also speaking French.

I remember when I realized I had left my briefcase in my boyfriend's truck, which had just traveled four hours away from me. I was surprised and ecstatic when he drove it all the way back to me the next day. It was a special delivery (a special doing) that really told me I was loved.

On the other hand, the Doer also uses their language to communicate the opposite of love. When the Doer is mad at you there are two things that will likely happen. One, he won't do anything for you, or two, he will actually make more work for you to do.

When a Doer Is Angry

If he is angry with you, that garbage can be over-flowing with stench and he will not take it out. That dead light bulb can sit for three weeks and he won't change it. Or he will open up a can of soup and leave it for you to pick up, rinse out, and throw away. He may leave the toilet seat up or down (as the case may be!), or his wet towel on the floor.

He is telling you loud and clear that he is not happy with you. He is speaking his language to communicate with you. If you are married to a Doer and you never do things for him, you are essentially saying, "I don't love you. I am mad at you. I don't care." That is what you are saying to them whether you are actually mad at them or not. That is how he interprets what you are not doing.

Just as languages have different dialects, silent languages do also. For example, those who grew up in Northern Ireland speak English; however, it sounds completely different from someone who grew up in Northern Michigan. As a Doer, you may care less about getting help carrying in the groceries, but if no one in the house ever helps to walk the dog you may not feel loved.

As a Doer I am often compelled to ask for the people in my life to do stuff: start my car, get the groceries, fold the laundry, pick this up, etc. When they do what I've asked, at an unconscious level, I feel loved.

You may be in relationship with a Doer who speaks loud and clear to you.

Is your husband a Doer? Are you?

What the Doer Complains About

If your husband always complaining and nagging, "You never take out the garbage. You never pick up after yourself, I need your help," and if he is complaining about what you do or don't do all the time, it is highly probable that their dominant silent language is Doer. Sometimes there are silent language clues in the words people choose to use or in their subject matter. The Doer's conversation will typically center on what someone did or did not do, or what someone is doing or not doing, or what he is going to do. He will ask what you are doing or what you are going to do. He can be irritated that you don't want to do the same thing he wants to do. He'll talk about helping others, too. And if you have promised to help them or do something and, in fact, you do not, they will be deeply affected in a negative way.

The Gifter

"All this I have spoken while still with you.
But the Counselor, the Holy Spirit, whom
the Father will send in my name, will teach you
all things and will remind you of everything

I have said to you. Peace I leave with you;
my peace I give you. I do not give to you
as the world gives."
−John 14:25-27a

Jesus as The Gifter gave us the ultimate gift!

The Gifter and Love

You can often tell who the Gifters are. They rarely forget a birthday. The Gifter is someone who, when they want to say "I love you" will give something to you. When you go shopping with a Gifter, they always have their radar set for presents for the next gift-giving holiday. They will say things such as "Joe would love that. I will get that for him for Christmas. Oh, Suzie would look so good in that. I think I'll pick it up for her." The Gifter is always thinking of what they can get someone else. It makes them feel so good to give.

The Gifter is a master at giving the perfect gift. They have a special sense about what their intended recipient would absolutely love. They will do everything they can to get that perfect gift for you. If someone in the Gifter's world gives them a well-thought-out gift, the Gifter feels good on the inside. The person who gave has spoken the Gifter's language and, thus, touched their heart deeply. They feel loved. Basically, a Gifter knows what item you need.

When a Gifter Is Angry

On the other hand, the Gifter can also use their dominant language to communicate the opposite of love. When the Gifter is angry with you, one of two things may occur. They won't give you a gift or the gift they give won't be up to their usual standards. It will be late, or it won't be wrapped. It is often very difficult for the Gifter to not give a gift, mostly because it has already been purchased way ahead of time. Gifters will generally have their Christmas presents purchased by October.

Gifters don't necessarily always like to receive gifts. Don't be confused. You would think that a person who speaks the Gifter language would love to get presents. However, when a Gifter gets a gift, because it is their silent language, they are very sensitive about whether someone really took the time to pick out the right, perfect gift.

My grandmother was a Gifter. She loved to give gifts. Christmas at her house was wall-to-wall presents everywhere. One year my grandpa got my grandma, who was short and plump, a great big black fur coat. My grandma was totally disgusted with my grandpa's present because it was something that she would never want. It made her skin crawl to put it on. My grandpa just thought, "I will spend money on Grandma and that will make her happy." A Gifter is very particular and sensitive about whether you put an effort into getting them the present they desire. When my grandpa had a diamond ring made especially for her, she was ecstatic. He got it right. He thought it through for her, and it spoke volumes of love to her. That gift meant everything in the whole world to her. With Gifters you really need to put some thought into the gift.

A client told me about her sister who behaved like a perfect example of a Gifter who is not happy with a loved one. When my friend and her family went to her sister's house last Christmas, in the hall closet where they put their coats, piled to the ceiling were exquisitely wrapped, ornate presents that were a feast for the eyes. After dinner, everyone went to the living room to open presents, but the sister walked into the kitchen, wrote checks, and proceeded to pass them out flippantly to several family guests, before passing out beautiful presents to the rest of her family members. This sister speaks the Gifter language. She was not happy with the people she tossed checks to.

She was silently speaking her language to tell them she was unhappy with them. She hadn't gone shopping to get and wrap the perfect gift for each of them as she did for all of the recipients of the presents in the closet and the other family members in the room that night. She was saying, "I am mad at you. I am not happy with you." You can always know when a Gifter is angry with you because they will skimp. Gifters have a hard time not giving at least something to a loved one, even if they are angry with them.

What the Gifter Complains About

If a significant person in your world is always complaining and nagging, it is a sure sign they are frustrated and they are feeling unloved. They will say things like, "You never remember my birthday! You never give me anything. You never bring me flowers. You are so selfish." Gifters are going to complain when they don't receive or they see others not giving and their conversation will often be centered on gifting subjects.

The Hugger

"They came to Bethsaida, and some people brought a blind man and begged Jesus to touch him. He took the blind man by the hand and led him outside the village. When he had spit on the man's eyes and put his hands on him, Jesus asked, 'Do you see anything?' He looked up and said, 'I see people; they look like trees walking around.' Once more Jesus put his hands on the man's eyes. Then his eyes were opened, his sight was restored, and he saw everything clearly."
–Mark 8:22-25

Jesus the Hugger, put his hand on them and they are healed.

The Hugger and Love

The Hugger is someone, who, when he wants to say "I love you" will hug you or reach out to touch you. When you run into a Hugger friend at the store, he will reach out to shake your hand, or give you a hug. If a Hugger really wants to make sure that you understand him or that he understood you, he'll tap you on the shoulder or hand so as to be sure to make a connection.

Huggers are happy when they touch, when they hug. It makes them feel incredible. When you are in a romantic relationship with a Hugger, the Hugger will be sitting at the table with their knee touching yours. Or on the couch watching TV, they will be holding hands, snuggling. You know, they have to be touching. It is something that just makes them feel great. Basically, a Hugger knows how you are feeling.

When a Hugger Is Angry

When a Hugger is angry with you, they may resort to not hugging or not touching you at all. They may make a point to stay away from you when they are mad at you. No touching.

They can also use the complete opposite of a hug to tell you they are mad at you. They may be someone with a tendency to hit the person they are angry with. You see, touching really means something to them. If they are furious with you, they may hit you, because that kind of touch really speaks their anger for them. It is their silent language and they are speaking it loud and clear.

Dialects come into play with the Hugger as well. If you really enjoy hugs and touching from your loved ones, but you must have your "space" while sleeping, you may have the Hugger as your dominant language. Remember, touch is very important to you, so the specific way you are touched and hugged may speak volumes to you.

What the Hugger Complains About

If a Hugger is not getting hugs or physical contact, they are feeling unloved. They will complain, "You never hug me. You never want hold hands. You never want to snuggle with me." The Hugger's conversation will often revolve around what things feel like and they will use feeling words to describe situations. For example, "Her attitude was prickly." Huggers can be irritated that you don't feel the same way about something as they do.

The Knower

> *"Knowing their thoughts, Jesus said, 'Why do you entertain evil thoughts in your hearts? Which is easier: to say, 'Your sins are forgiven,' or to say, 'Get up and walk?' But so that you may know that the Son of Man has authority on earth to forgive sins...' Then he said to the paralytic,*

'Get up, take your mat and go home.' And the man got up and went home. When the crowd saw this, they were filled with awe; and they praised God, who had given such authority to men."
–Matthew 9:4-8

Jesus the Knower knows what is needed heals them.

The Knower can pick up on someone else's energy or vibe easily. When they want to let you know they love you, they will know how to make you happy. It is the sensory language that we all speak where we have a sense about things, about where other people are at emotionally. A stranger may walk into the room and a Knower will know immediately or get a good sense of whether that person is "bad" or creepy, dishonest or is presenting himself under false pretenses. They can also immediately get a sense if someone is good and has good intentions. You may have been in a meeting or a classroom and had the vibe that a person didn't care or like you very much even though verbally they never told you so. Basically, a Knower is pretty good at knowing what you are thinking.

The Knower and Love

We speak the Knower language very eloquently when we love someone in a spiritual sense. We think happy and nice loving thoughts of them. We think about the happy future with them. When we do this, we are sending good energy towards them and the next time we connect, it's like those happy thoughts paved the way for even more happiness. Even from a distance, the Knower can sense that they are loved and being loved. Know that they are being thought of in-kind regard.

When the Knower Is Angry

When we are very angry at someone as a Knower we can be sending out negative angry energy to them. When we finally connect with them, all heck breaks loose because spiritually the tension has been building up. I had a client who would know when the tires of her husband's Suburban hit the gravel at the end of the driveway if he was coming home drunk or not.

We can use our happy Knowing spirit and our angry Knowing spirit to say "I love you" or "I can't stand you." Without ever saying a word, parents especially can use their Knower language to communicate that they love and are happy with you, and they can use it to say "I am really angry with you and you are bad." The Knower's words can be used as either a sword or a comfortable pillow.

What the Knower Complains About

Knowers complain about you not "knowing" or sensing things that they easily and clearly "know" and sense. They will say things like, "You couldn't tell he wasn't to be trusted? You didn't know I was only thinking of you? You should have just known!" "How could you not know I was mad at you?" They also get very angry if they are left out of the loop in planning. They need to know everything.

Conversation is usually centered on what "they know" or what someone else knew or didn't know.

The Looker

"Then He said to Thomas, 'Reach your finger here, and look at My hands; and reach your hand here, and put it into My side. Do not be unbelieving, but believing.'"
–John 20:27

Jesus the Looker had us look and we believed.

The Looker and Love

How things "look" is the Looker's top priority. When they want to tell you they love you, they will make things look good. They are overly concerned about how you look, what you're wearing, how high your heels are, wrinkles, and symmetry. They get overly worked up about how they imagine they look to the outside world. Many of my students have associated this silent language with Obsessive Compulsive Disorder. I tend to agree with them; however, you can be a Looker and not be obsessive.

They might color-coordinate their outfits (or yours). When things look good, it makes them feel good. How things look is what a Looker talks about all the time. They will be very opinionated about how things look on a constant basis. They will say things like "That looks terrible," or "That looks pretty." They will notice when things are moved or have been visually changed in some way. Basically a Looker knows how things need to look.

When a Looker Is Angry

When a Looker is angry with you, they will, on purpose, make things not look good because they think it will tell you that they are unhappy with you. They will leave the house a mess, or if they are really angry, they may damage something of yours so it doesn't look good anymore. They may, for example, key your vehicle, break something, or punch a hole in the wall. That way it won't look good anymore, effectively telling you "I'm mad at you." It is all about how things look.

What the Looker Complains About

Lookers will complain about things not looking "good enough," and they will be irritated with you if you do not put the same high priority on things looking good.

They will be irritated that you don't "see" the same as they "see."

The Spotlighter

> *"When the apostles returned, they reported to Jesus what they had done. Then He took them with Him and they withdrew by themselves to a town called Bethsaida, but the crowds learned about it and followed Him. He welcomed them and spoke to them about the kingdom of God, and healed those who needed healing."*
> –Luke 9:10-11

Jesus the Spotlighter spends time with people and they are healed.

The Spotlighter and Love

The Spotlighter really likes to have eyes on them. When they want to tell you they love you, they will be with you and spend time with you. They either like to be in the spotlight or they so greatly avoid being in the spotlight that they actually become spotlighted. More on the latter later.

Spotlighters love to play games. Card games, board games, ballgames, and the like because they get one-on-one eye contact with you. They just feel totally loved.

You can often see it in children. If their dominant desire is for you to watch them, Spotlighters will say "Watch me, Mommy," "Watch me, Daddy." I had one client tell me that her young son came to her one day, put both hands on her cheeks, looked her in the eyes and said, "Mommy! Watch me!" That was a pretty good indication that her son is a Hugger and a Spotlighter.

Another client of mine said, "I think my son is a Spotlighter because it is not okay for me to be doing the dishes while he is reading to me at the kitchen table. He wants me to just sit with him and watch him read. It is not okay to be doing both jobs." She loved that she learned the seven silent languages because now she can speak his native tongue. While she is watching him read, she knows she is also giving him the love he is seeking. This actually allows her to get more done because she gives full attention to her son making him not as needy. Basically, the Spotlighter really wants eyes on them.

There are many actors and actresses who love the spotlight on them because it makes them feel loved. Some Spotlighters will often speak loudly or dress in such a way as to draw attention to them. Teachers are often Spotlighters. They love being at the head of the class with eyes on them. Incidentally, sometimes it is why the classroom rebel and the teacher have such great strife. The teacher and the problem student are vying for the center of attention.

Everybody grows up with a Spotlighter. There are always a couple of Spotlighters in any class. You remember those kids who would always raise their hands with the answer to a question. They were pumped up by having the attention of the teacher and the class. Remember the kid who got attention by acting out and making noises or talking when the teacher was talking. They get pumped up when people look at them or notice they are different. They may shy away and always try not to be "in the group" or they may dress like no one else. Either way they are getting eyes on them.

Some Spotlighters are not concerned about what kind of energy is behind the eyes that are looking at them. It makes no difference if the eyes are looking at them in anger or if the eyes are looking at them in love. They get a sense of being pumped up as long as eyes are on them.

A student in my class sat down, covered his eyes with his ball cap, and leaned back as though he were going to sleep. He was always working very hard not be like the other students. This behavior alerted me that he was a Spotlighter. I was sure to always look him in the eyes every chance he would give me. One night about three weeks after I taught the class on silent languages, he hung back after class to tell me about how he recognized the silent languages in his parents and himself.

He went on to tell me about how he was expelled from school in the seventh grade for vying for attention and that it was such a traumatic experience for the teacher that she retired and he never returned to school. If she had known about the silent languages, I wonder if things might have turned out differently for both of them.

When you get into an argument with a Spotlighter, they will chase you down the hallway to argue with you because they want your eyes. It is super important. They won't stop until they get your eyes and they will try to keep your eyes for as long as possible. It can be so exhausting if you don't speak the language.

I had a student who recognized that his father is a Spotlighter. His dad was always lecturing him. His dad would tirelessly go on and on, and the moment his son would look him in the eyes and acknowledge what he was saying, his dad would stop. The son played his dad like a fiddle. However, the son was also a Spotlighter. While the dad was essentially begging his son's attention, the son was getting the eyes of his father the whole time, which, unconsciously, is what the son really wanted.

When a Spotlighter Is Angry

Spotlighters will tell you they are unhappy with you by not spending time with you. If you suddenly stop getting invited to do something with a Spotlighter, they are probably telling you they are not so happy with you.

Do you know someone who is estranged from their loved one? They don't speak to a friend or family member for years. They refuse to go to events where a certain family member or ex-friend is going to be. Have you noticed that this is their standard method of communicating they are angry with someone? A Spotlighter can leave behind a long trail of people over the years. They are speaking loud and clear that they are angry.

What the Spotlighter Complains About

Spotlighters complain "You never want to spend time with me."

I was very surprised to discover that on average seventy percent of my inmate students are Spotlighters. I thought that was so strange because being in jail minimizes the quality time they have with loved ones. I discovered jail supplies them with their much-desired "eyes on them." Inmates are on camera 24/7! The whole family is on schedule waiting for the inmates' planned phone calls home. They get letters from loved ones where they know that the author spent their "time-on-them" in writing.

When the kids are getting tucked in, unconsciously, the inmate knows that they are missed and being thought of. Friends and family are often praying for them. The Spotlighter knows, unconsciously, that because they are missing from the "party," they are actually being thought of and talked about. However, when the inmate gets home it is not all about them anymore. Spotlighter inmates, unconsciously, know how to get the attention they crave. They just do something to get in trouble again.

Tantrums are another tool that Spotlighters use to get attention. If tantrums worked for getting attention when they were children, many Spotlighters have "grown-up" tantrums as adults. It's harder for Spotlighters to grow out of tantrums because yelling and screaming and giant attitude problems get eyes on them. Why should they stop? They are getting what they need.

The Worder

*"When Jesus had entered Capernaum,
a centurion came to him, asking for help.
'Lord,' he said, 'my servant lies at home
paralyzed and in terrible suffering.' Jesus
said to him, 'I will go and heal him.' The
centurion replied, 'Lord, I do not deserve
to have you come under my roof. But just
say the word, and my servant will be
healed....' Then Jesus said to the
centurion, 'Go! It will be done just
as you believed it would.' And his servant
was healed at that very hour."*
–Matthew 8:5-8 and 13

Jesus the Worder gave the word and the servant was healed.

The Worder and Love

The last silent language is the Worder. It's not quite so silent, but if Worder is your most dominant silent language you are extremely effective at using words for loving and hating. Let's notice how a Worder silently communicates love.

You can tell if you are a Worder because you always have a kind word to say. You are very encouraging with words. You love greeting cards that say just the right thing, just the right way. You enjoy spending time finding just the right card. You probably also love books, and you pay attention when someone recommends one.

When Worders notice you, they affirm you with their words! Worders get pumped up when someone notices them and affirms or encourages them, especially if the words are carefully chosen.

When a Worder Is Angry

If you are a Worder, and you are angry with someone, it is very likely that you will use your words to tell them so. You are extremely skillful at speaking the most hurtful words that cut a person like a knife. The other thing a Worder will do when they are mad is they will not speak words to you. They give you the silent treatment because they have had the silent treatment used on them and it drives them crazy. By wielding the silent treatment, they intend to devastate you as much as the silent treatment devastates them. By not speaking to a Worder, you speak directly to their core: "I am not happy with you."

Worders are very good with words. They remember lyrics to songs. You know how some songs have words that you can't quite make out? Well, the Worder will instinctively know what those words are. They remember exactly what someone said and they can correct you with the right words verbatim. They understand puns and how politicians or preachers use words for effect.

What the Worder Complains About

Worders complain with sentences like, "You never talk to me anymore" or "You never notice that I did a good job." Or "You never tell me I look pretty." Worders need compliments to get a sense of love. They also complain, loud and clear, when they give you the silent treatment. Their relationships are centered on conversations. They remember them. They never forget them and they cherish the good ones. They get irritated if you don't like to spend time talking. Worders are okay with spending time talking on the phone.

Silent Languages Can Be Tricky

From a Gifter to a Worder

A client asked her husband what his silent language was. He thought he was a Gifter because his parents were Gifters and it made him feel good when they gave gifts to him. He gives gifts to tell people he loves them because that was modeled to him. Over time, however, my girlfriend noticed that his true silent language was Worder. He gave gifts to say, "I love you," but what he was really looking for were words. She is now sure to give him just the right words of appreciation for the gifts she receives from him.

From a Doer to a Spotlighter

You may recall my boyfriend is a Hugger and a Doer, or so I thought. While I was writing this book, I discovered his real dominant silent language. Late one afternoon, I started deep cleaning his bathroom from ceiling to floor, every nook and cranny. Hours later, I found him on the couch with a not-so-happy attitude. He was upset that I spent all the time cleaning instead of spending time with him before I headed back home where we wouldn't be able to see each other for a few weeks. He spoke his dominant silent language to me loud and clear. He is a Spotlighter. I discovered he does things in order to be with the ones he loves. A Doer would have been absolutely ecstatic that the bathroom was getting done!

Remember the story earlier about how my boyfriend brought me my briefcase that I left in his truck? He drove four hours to return it to me and I thought he did that for me as a Doer. Actually, he was speaking his Spotlighter language to me, spending time with me.

Knowing Your Silent Language Helps You Love as Jesus Would

When my daughter was about three years old we were shopping at the grocery store. She caught sight of, and wanted me to buy her, a six-dollar "Strawberry Patch" coloring book! I thought, "I am not wasting my money on a coloring book." (Remember, Gifting is not my key language.) I told her no. She was devastated. I didn't get just how devastated.

One summer my daughter was just not happy in her interactions with me. Very often she kept hurting me. I know that she wasn't hurting me on purpose. However, she kept stepping on my feet, elbowing me, shaking a sandy towel right next to me… on and on it went. After so long I knew she was, unconsciously, angry with me. She was speaking her dominant language to tell me she wasn't happy with me. It kept happening until finally she nailed me in the tummy with an elbow, and I realized, "Okay, this has got to stop!" So, I put her on my lap.

(Note how I used our common Hugger language.) I said, "Honey, what is so wrong, why are you so mad at me?" She said, with her bottom lip quivering, "You didn't buy me the coloring book at the grocery store!" Tears filled her eyes and I gave her a big hug. I told her I was sorry, that I didn't realize it was so important to her. She looked at me and said, "Does that mean I can have the coloring book?" I said, "No, but what it does mean is that I will be more aware of what it is that you need from me next time. I will be better at it for you."

I get her now. I speak her language. When she was three years old she believed that when I got her a gift I was telling her I loved her, and when I didn't give her a gift I was telling her I didn't love her. Now she knows that isn't true.

This Is How to Live and Love

Now that you know about these silent languages, when you interact with your husband whom you love, you know how to speak to him in his natural tongue. If you are in a relationship with a Worder, speak words that lift him up. If wording is at the bottom of your list, because you love him, make a point to tell him how wonderful he is in your world and how much you appreciate him. You will be surprised how fantastic you feel after speaking in someone's silent language, even if it is not your own! It may be that you are a Gifter, but if you want both of you to experience a terrific relationship, don't bring them flowers if gifting is not their dominant language! See how we use these silent languages to pump each other up and tear each other down?

Don't speak Spanish to someone who speaks French. We make relationships work when we speak the same language. Listen to what they are complaining about because they are speaking in their dominant language. If they say "You never say anything nice," they are probably a Worder. If they complain "You never spend time with me," they are probably a Spotlighter. If you hear "You never hold my hand," they are probably a Hugger.

Give gifts to the Gifters in your life. Give words to the Worders in your life. Give time to your Spotlighters.

Now that you understand the seven silent languages and how you use them in relationships to make your world better or perpetuate misery, you can see how we use all the silent languages to say "I love you" as well as "I am not happy with you." However, one or two silent languages will surface for you. You won't have to work at speaking them. We all do things for others. We all give gifts. We all hug people. We all like to have someone notice us. We all like to say nice things to people, and we all like to have someone say nice things to us. We all like things to look nice. We all have a sense of whether someone is happy with us or unhappy with us, and we tell people, using silent negative energy and attitude, that we are happy or unhappy with them.

Need help determining what your husband's silent language is? Go to www.christianwomansguide.com/silent for a list of common words used in conversation that can help identify your husband's dominant language.

CHAPTER 8

The Law of Reflection and the Epiphany Approach

"Then you shall see and be radiant; your heart
shall throb and swell with joy."
–Isaiah 60:5

There is a law at work in your life you have known about through God's word. It is the common denominator for absolutely everything you have gone through. Once you are exposed to the reality of it, your relationship with yourself, your husband, your children, your boss, your mother, sister, brother, neighbor, and friend will never be quite the same. It's the Law of

Reflection (LOR) and it's summed up in Matthew 12:34, *"For out of the abundance of the heart that the mouth speaks."* It is the most pivotal of all scripture regarding your troublesome marriage. For my clients, this is the scripture which has transformed their relationships with their husbands the most.

I love to consider also that the Lord does not look at the things man looks at. Man looks at the outward appearance, but the Lord looks at the heart. (1 Samuel 16:7b) God created us in His image as we discussed earlier. That means you can do some things like He does. Therefore, if you decide to look at things of the heart and He told you that out of the overflow of his heart his mouth speaks, then you should be able to know your man's heart.

The LOR is the idea that what you are experiencing in front of you is a reflection of what is inside of you, and is in direct alignment with scripture. *"You, therefore, have no excuse, you who pass judgment on someone else, for at whatever point you judge the other, you are condemning yourself, because you who pass judgment do the same things."* (Romans 2:1) *"Do you have contempt for God, who is very kind to you, puts up with you, and deals patiently with you? Don't you realize that it is God's kindness that is trying to lead you to Him and change the way you think and act?"* (Romans 2:4) God uses the LOR, or the parables in your life, to lead you to exactly what you need repentance for! *"Therefore no one will be declared righteous in His sight by observing the law [Such as the Ten Commandments and others], rather through the law we become conscious of sin."* (Rom 3:20)

If you filter what happens and your opinion of what happened through the LOR, you become more deeply conscious of our own particular sin. You get to see, hear, and understand the specific nature of your sin that the Holy Spirit desires you to work on. When you do this, the law is manifested inside your heart and responds in love; which is really why the law was created.

God Speaks to Us in Parables, Today

"Then he told them many things in parables saying, 'A farmer went out to sow his seed. As he was scattering the seed some fell along the path, and the birds came and ate it up. Some fell on rocky places, where it did not have much soil. It sprang up quickly because the soil was shallow. But when the sun came up, the plants were scorched, and they withered because they had no root. Other seed fell among thorns, which grew up and choked the plants. Still other seed fell on good soil, where it produced a crop—a hundred, sixty or thirty times what was sown. He who has ears, let him hear.' The disciples came to him and asked, 'Why do you speak to the people in parables?' He replied, 'The knowledge of the secrets of the kingdom of heaven has been given to you, but not to them. Whoever has will be given more, and he will have

an abundance. Whoever does not have, even what he has will be taken from him. This is why I speak to them in parables. Though seeing, they do not see; though hearing, they do not hear or understand.'" (Matthew 1:3-13)

"You will be ever hearing but never understanding; you will be ever seeing but never perceiving. For this people's heart has become calloused; they hardly hear with their ears, and they have closed their eyes. Otherwise they might see with their eyes, hear with their ears, and understand with their hearts and turn, and I would heal them." (Matthew 13:14-15) Jesus described what the parable meant in detail because they asked. He will do the same for us when we ask. Especially, now that he is seated at the right hand of the Father and lives in us and has given us His Holy Spirit!

My question to you is, "What if the person in front of you is your parable direct from God about what He wants you to know about you?" For example, your husband comes in the house screaming at you for "not following through." Using what God told you that, *"out of the overflow of his heart his mouth speaks"* (Luke 6:45b), you can be confident that in at least one area of his life he isn't following through. Based on my experience, it also means that on the inside of himself he is using the same tone of voice and the same intensity with himself over the fact that he is not following through. You are just showing up to show him himself.

Of course, there is your role in this matter as well—your parable. If you are upset that he said that and feel unjustly accused so you yell right back and self-righteously list all the things you have followed through on in an indignant tone, then there is probably some place where you are not following through, too.

By going in and asking God to help you see, you now have the keys to process your circumstances and the people in your life. This way, forgiving someone is not as hard. You're not forgiving that person with a grumbling heart or out of obligation to God, but through a tender heart of understanding, really a heart of gratitude for that person coming into your life to show what you're doing to yourself.

The Epiphany Approach

It is very advantageous to filter everything that someone says or does through the Epiphany Approach because what you are experiencing in front of you is a reflection of something going on inside of you. To use the Epiphany Approach, you ask yourself "How is it that I do that to me? How is it that I do that to them?" By asking ourselves these questions, we will always be hearing and understanding. We will always be seeing and perceiving. For those in Christ, we will become tenderhearted; precisely hearing with our ears and clearly seeing with our eyes.

"Be on your guard against the yeast of the Pharisees, which is hypocrisy. There is NOTHING concealed that will not be disclosed, or hidden that will not be made known. What you have said in the dark will be heard in the daylight, and what you have whispered in the ear in the inner rooms will be proclaimed from the roofs." (Luke 12:2-3) Nothing. There is not a single thing that will not be made known. You proclaim your own issues from the rooftops every time you open your mouth and so does your husband! The Epiphany Approach will show you how this is true and how you can transform your relationship by acting as Jesus would.

I am going to tell you a story of what happened to me. Then I'll take you through my story again as I reveal the Epiphany Approach. It is a six-step process that reveals what God wants to show me so I can transform the situation. First, I notice the reflection, then notice my opinion. Next, I commune with God and get the Epiphany. Then I express my appreciation to God for the big reveal and finally I make a decision to either preserve the situation so it will keep happening or to transform, giving me a greater chance for changing the situation.

He Broke His Promise to Me!

My son just swooped in from college. I have spent about two hours with him in three months. He promised me we would spend time together when he came in to town. Twice he has been into town and the "spent time" was mere minutes. I was ticked. I had that agitated feeling going on inside of me. That negative feeling lets you know that what is playing out on the outside of you is actually happening on the inside of you first. "He broke his promise to me", I said.

"So, Lord, where is it that I have broken my promise to me," I asked.

There it was. Immediately I knew what it was. I had committed myself to getting this book published by June. It's the seventeenth of June and I am still in the writing phase. I am nowhere near even editing yet. My heart is glad to know this because I can do something about this. I can't make my son hang out with me. Thank you, Jesus.

I cannot make other people keep their promises, but I do have control over whether I keep my promises to myself. God, then, takes care of the rest. As I keep my promises to myself and of course to other people, God sends people to me that keep their promises.

He Broke His Promise to Me, Dissected Through the Epiphany Approach

REFLECTION: Twice he has been into town and the "spent time" was mere minutes. I was ticked. I had that agitated feeling going on inside of me

OPINION: "He broke his promise to me", I said.

COMMUNION: "So, Lord, where is it that I have broken my promise to me," I asked.

EPIPHANY: There it was. Immediately I knew what it was. I had committed myself to getting this book published by June. It's the seventeenth of June and I am still in the writing phase. I am nowhere near even editing yet.

APPRECIATION: Thank you, Jesus.

DECISION: Two choices—Preservation or Transformation

Preservation:

I can do nothing. Just keep on not working on my book. I can keep thinking that my son is the one with the problem of not keeping his promises and go crazy trying to make him do what I want him to do. All the while God will keep bringing people and circumstances into my world that prove people don't keep their promises. Remember our God is the God of Peter, Jonah, Mark, Samson, and David who all received second and even many more chances. He will continue to give you second chances because it is another chance for you to go in and get close to Him.

Transformation:

The best way to stop someone from breaking their promises to me is to follow through with my own commitments to myself. My outside, their broken promises to me, reflected my inside, broken promises to myself. This is how you know that in all things God works for the good of those who love Him and have been called according to his purpose. Every moment of your life has the sole purpose for you to be in communion with Him.

Get Answers

Truly, I say to you, that even if you stop and ask God, "How is this (whatever you don't like) a reflection of me?" That pause, when you wait for the answer, is you really connecting with that part of you where Jesus lives. He wants you to know the answer to that question. After all, He said in Matthew 7:7, *"Ask and you shall receive."* The outcome of your behavior after receiving the answer is that you will respond as Jesus would. Of course, He is going to reveal it to you. It will heal you. In John 10:10 He also said, *"I have come that they may have life and have it to the full."* I say, if you ask Him, *"How is it that I do that very thing to me?"* He will absolutely answer you because you can change that. Go in.

I Screw Myself Over!

REFLECTION: Another comment by a client tells all, "Well, I'm not screwing every girl in the park, like he is!"
OPINION: I asked "So, go in and ask God [COMMUNION] what girl have you been screwing over again and again?"
EPIPHANY: She buried her face in her hands.

APPRECIATION: "It's cool God told you that, yes? Now tell me, is the same intensity that you are angry at him for what he has done, *the same intensity* that you are angry with yourself? Tell me, how often are you doing this to you?"

"Every time I find out about his unfaithfulness, I screw myself over by going back to him."

DECISION: I advised, "This is the pivotal point where you can choose to do the same thing which assures you will get the same result (Preservation), or you can choose to not go back with him (Transformation). Keep in mind that the more you take care of you the more likely it is that God will bring someone into your life who cares for you and loves you and respects you because you are respecting and loving yourself. It is very attractive."

Whoever Accepts

In John 13:20, Jesus said, "*I tell you the truth, whoever accepts anyone I send accepts me; and whoever accepts me accepts the one who sent me.*" The word "anyone" in this scripture is very intriguing. How do we know if the person in front of us is from Jesus or not? Is there any way to know for sure? Grappling around and around with this, it made sense to just decide that anyone in front of me at any given moment was specifically sent to me by Jesus and most importantly by accepting them

I was, in turn, accepting Jesus Himself and the message He has for me though them.

Two things to point out here. 1) Heart or attitude is very important because God knows our hearts so if we "accept" the person with a grumbling heart we really are not accepting them at all. You know it. God knows it. And guess what? That person knows it, senses it, or feels it as well. 2) If we are to accept anyone He sends, then it is reasonable to believe that they may have a message for us direct from our creator. Does this feel right to you?

If someone comes up to you and gives you a hug or tells you what a good job you did, it is easy to see how that could possibly be a message sent from God. However, if someone comes to you and says in a loud angry voice, "You dropped the ball," this is a tougher concept to get a handle on, that God is sending you a message in that manner. But what if we were to filter the message through the Law of Reflection. What you are experiencing in front of you is a reflection of what is inside of you. One way to look at it is to ask, "What is my opinion of that person speaking to me in that way?" For example, "They are avoiding responsibility and blaming others." Go inside and ask God, "How is it exactly or where is it exactly that I am avoiding responsibility by blaming someone else? I am willing to bet that you have been using the same tone of voice with yourself over the issue.

As You Judge, You Will Be Judged

Matthew 7:2, "*For in the same way you judge others, you will be judged, and with the measure you use it will be measured to you.*"

God wanted you to know about you, so He sent them, every single one of them. Accept them and the message they have for you. Accept them because their message for you is really for them, too! This is how we accept Jesus. It is how we get to behave like Jesus. It is how we get to be like Jesus within our realm of influence.

He Calls Me a Game Playing Crazy Person

Another way to look at the Epiphany Approach is to look at what is on the outside of you and make a judgment about what is really going on with someone else. Use what they say to understand what is going on in their heart.

I have had clients in my office who are angry because their husband is calling them names.

"He calls me a game-playing crazy person."

I replied, "If it is true that your outside is a reflection of your inside, tell me, where is your husband coming from on the inside of him?"

"That somewhere on the inside of him he knows he is playing games and is crazy."

"Does that sound about right," I asked?

"Yes, definitely!"

Know that beyond a shadow of a doubt. He is even using the same tone of voice within himself and he is saying it with the same emotional intensity about himself. Whether he will get quiet enough to understand that about himself is not for you to figure out. It is your job, if it bothers you that he is talking to you like that, to go in and ask the Lord where that statement is true about you, so that it can't sting you anymore!

Just Ask

"Jesus answered, 'I am the way, the truth, and the life. No one comes to the Father except through me. If you really knew me, you would know my Father as well. From now on, you do know him and have seen him.' Philip said, 'Lord, show us the Father and that will be enough for us.' Jesus answered, 'Don't you know me, Philip, even after I have been among you such a long time? Anyone who has seen me has seen the Father. How can you say, 'show us the Father?' Don't you believe that I am in the Father, and that the Father is in me? The words I say to you are not just my own. Rather, it is the Father, living in me, who is doing His work. Believe me when I say that I am in the Father and the Father is in me; or at least believe on the evidence of the miracles themselves. I tell you the truth, anyone who has faith in me will do what I have been doing. He will do even greater things than these, because I am going to the

Father. And I will do whatever you ask in my name, so that the son may bring glory to the Father. You may ask me for anything in my name and I will do it. If you love me, you will obey what I command.'" (John 14: 6-15)

Wait a minute, what did He just command, twice in a row? Ask him for anything and he'll do it in order to bring glory to the Father. Even if you believe He will only do some of what you ask Him, it would seem reasonable that if you wanted to love the person He sent to you in their sin or meanness or thoughtlessness or however they showed up and you asked "how is it that I do that to me" or "how is it that I act that way to myself" or "where is it that I use that tone of voice with myself," it just seems that would be an asking that Jesus would answer—because the truth will set you free—free to love one another.

"If you really knew me, you would know my Father as well." If we really want to know Jesus, we will see the people He sends to us to be the image of or manifestation of what He wants us to know and that will mean that from now on, we will know Him and have seen Him.

Jesus goes on to say, *"The words I say to you are not just my own. Rather it is the Father living in me, who is doing the work. Anyone who has seen me has seen the Father.*

Now we see but a poor reflection as in a mirror; then we shall see face to face. Now I know in part, then I shall know fully, even as I am fully known." (1Corinthians 13:12)

Who Does God's Work?

Who is doing his work? Even if you can't imagine in your wildest dreams your husband who is being so nasty to you has God in him, at least you can muster up the understanding that there may be a message for you from God. Use your opinion of him to discover the very personal message sent directly to you through this person. God can use people and circumstances for His purposes, right?

Your husband says to you, "What's your problem?" in a mean grumbling voice. What do you know about him? Yes, that he has a problem. In that moment he speaks those words, you can take it on truth that he is the one with a problem, for sure! For it is written, *"for a tree is recognized by its fruit."* (Matthew 12:33b)

He's an Idiot

Your outside is a reflection of your inside. Does your husband always call you a name? Like "You're an idiot!" "You idiot! You left the door open!" "Who's the idiot who thought that up?" "Don't be an idiot!" "That was an idiotic thing to do!" Okay now go back in your memory. Can you think of at least one time when he behaved like an idiot? What? You say, "MORE than one occasion?" Wrap your mind around this. For every time the comment was made there was a corresponding idiotic behavior, thought, or action by the person doing the exclaiming. *"You, therefore, have no excuse, you who pass judgment on someone else, for at whatever point you judge the other, you are condemning yourself, because you who pass judgment do the same things."* (Romans 2:2)

"He said to the crowd, 'When you see a cloud rising in the west, immediately you say, 'It's going to rain,' and it does. And when the south wind blows, you say it is going to be hot,' and it is. Hypocrites! You know how to interpret the appearance of the earth and the sky. How is it that you don't know how to interpret this present time?'" (Luke 12:54-56) He was calling us hypocrites because WE CAN INTERPRET this present time…and who is present before you at any given time! He follows that scripture with, *"Why don't you judge for yourselves what is right?"* (Luke 12:57) By considering your opinion (judgment) of your neighbor with the Epiphany Approach you are judging for yourself what is right. You can't change them, or the weather, but you can change you. Then your adversary will disappear. Remember Jesus said in Matthew 18:18, *"Truly I tell you, whatever you bind on earth will be bound in heaven, and whatever you loose on earth will be loosed in heaven."* Loose the malice and slander from within you and malice and slander will be loosed from your future experience.

I Stink?

I had student tell me, "Christine, I agree with you on most of what you said. But I don't agree with you that if someone stinks and that bothers me [REFLECTION] that I stink."

I replied, "Well, have you ever heard of stinkin' thinking?"

"Yeah, But... I still don't see it."

"Okay. How would you describe that person that stinks?"

"They neglect themselves [OPINION]. They don't care."

"Use those words to describe you. Go in and say, 'I am neglecting something that I should be taking care of.'" [COMMUNION]

"Oh! I get it now [EPIPHANY]," he said with a weary grin.

"Tell me what have you been neglecting that is stinking? And stinking may be a metaphor."

"Well what comes to my mind is I have been neglecting to eat healthy. Things just haven't been right with my digestion, stinky if you know what I mean. Wow! [APPRECIATION] "

"God will keep the stench on the outside of you until you take care of the stench on the inside of you. [DECISION]"

Judgement

"But I tell you that anyone who is angry with his brother will be subject to judgment." (Matthew 5:22)

"*Jesus says settle matters quickly with your adversary*" (Matthew 5:25) And, "*But I tell you; love your enemies and pray for those who persecute you.*" (Matthew 5:44) When your husband ticks you off ask, "How is it that I do that?" Discover it before he points it out to you, accuses you before you've had a chance to correct it. The Epiphany Approach allows you to settle matters quickly because you see what God sees. It is the most effective way to transform your heart toward your enemy with the added bonus of receiving the peace that surpasses all understanding. "*Do not be anxious about anything, but in everything, by prayer and petition, with thanksgiving, present your requests to God. And the peace of God, which transcends all understanding, will guard your hearts and minds in Christ Jesus.*" (Philippians 4:6-7)

It is interesting that Jesus talks for two pages straight in Matthew 5 through 6 about how we judge and are hypocrites, then in Chapter 7 he starts right out by saying, "*Do not judge, or you too will be judged. For in the same way you judge others, you will be judged, and with the measure you use, it will be measured to you.*" (Matthew 7:1)

Over time we can get to a state of mind that does not judge outwardly—and therefore we become the opposite of a hypocrite.

"*Why do you look at the speck of sawdust in your brother's eye and pay no attention to the plank in your own eye? How can you say to your brother, 'Let me take the speck out of your eye;' when all the time there is a plank in your own eye? You hypocrite, first take the plank out of your own eye, and then you will see clearly to remove the speck from your brother's eye."* (Matthew 7:3-5) He goes right into the solution, *"Ask and it will be given to you; seek and you will find; knock and the door will be opened to you. For everyone who asks receives; he who seeks finds; and to him who knocks, the door will be opened."* (Matthew 7:7-8)

As Jesus lives inside you, He is speaking to you in parables and metaphors all the time, 100% of the time, through what you hear and see. If you use the questions of The Epiphany Approach, "How is it that I do that to me? "How is it that I do that to them?", then, as a believer, you will always be hearing and understanding; always be seeing and perceiving. For those in Christ will become tenderhearted; precisely hearing with their ears and clearly seeing with their eyes. Asking the Epiphany questions inherently turns your heart toward Christ, toward healing, and thereby healing the entire world. For you are the only one who can change; for you are the only one who can decide not to conform any longer to the pattern of this world. But be transformed by the renewing of your mind. Then you will be able to test and approve what God's will is—*"His good, pleasing and perfect will."* (Romans 12:2)

The LOR is the method by which we can interpret the speck of sawdust in our brother's eye and determine exactly what the plank is in our own eye.

They're Selfish!

One inmate that attended my classes often came in with the same complaint about the people in his life [REFLECTION]. He said, "They're selfish. I give my brother cigarettes all the time and when I ask him for one, he says NO. I loaned my cousin money and when I asked to borrow money from him, he said NO. I have helped my friends move (one girl, I helped move twice) and when I needed help moving, none of them helped me. I have traded food with my cellmates and when I want to trade with them, they won't do it."

"How is it that *you* are selfish," I asked.

He sat forward in his chair and said with a stern voice, "I give people the shirt off my back and I get nothin' in return. I AM NOT SELFISH! [OPINION]"

"Okay," I said. "See if you can get quiet with you. Go inside of you and ask for God to show you where *you* are being selfish toward *you*. [COMMUNION]"

When he went in, I went in too, and God revealed to me that he had shifted from "they're selfish" to "I deserve."

I rephrased the question. "Do you agree that *you* deserved to be helped and traded with and so forth?"

He nodded.

"Where is it that *you* are not giving *you* what *YOU* really *deserve?*"

He sat back in his chair. A relaxed "knowing" came over him [EPIPHANY] and he said, "Freedom. I keep getting myself in trouble and locked up. I am keeping me away from my family and friends and what I love to do."

I said, "It's like hiding a favorite toy so no one else can have it, selfish."

Yes, "I am selfish because I keep making choices that don't give me freedom. Gosh, I never realized that." [APPRECIATION]

"What do you really desire? "

"Freedom."

"Ah, now you are at a pivotal choice [DECISION]. How is freedom attainable? "

"Not drink [Transformation]."

"And what happens if you drink [Preservation]?"

"I will be in jail, being selfish with me, with a bunch of selfish people."

"The choice is yours. As you start to be more generous to you, watch with delight as God brings more giving people into your world that reflect your new heart of generosity toward yourself."

In Romans 3:19-20 Paul says, *"Now we know that whatever the law says, it says to those who are under the law, so that every mouth may be silenced and the whole world held accountable to God. Therefore no one will be declared righteous in His sight by observing the law; rather, through the law we become conscious of sin."* If this scripture is filtered through the Epiphany Approach, you understand that God is using the people and circumstances of our lives to silence us, to go in, and allow God to hold us accountable. They are there to help us become conscious of our sin, too, like a parable.

"You, then, who teach others, do you not teach yourself?" (Romans 2:21a) As the author of this book I can certainly say, "Yes!" I for one have certainly experienced, and I bet you have as well, a time when I gave advice and realized that what was coming out of my mouth was actually advice meant for me. The difference here from the norm is that this is one hundred percent true— one-hundred percent of the time. You just have not been conscious of it until now. *"You who preach against stealing, do you steal?"* (Romans 2:21b) This is the same type of question that Jesus asked the people who were about to stone the adulterer. At some level, we do the same sin. What I am trying to impress upon you is this is absolute, steadfast truth. That what is going on outside of you and your opinions about that is what is going on inside of you and the only chance you have to make a positive impact on the situation is to recognize that. The struggle is not in how to get the other person to change, but rather the struggle is getting yourself to change—which is the only thing you have absolute power over anyway. If you are

a control freak, rejoice, because by controlling yourself, you will have much more control over your world. If you feel helpless to change your situation, rejoice because you now have the keys to the kingdom of heaven.

"Therefore no one will be declared righteous in His sight by observing the law [Such as the Ten Commandments and others], rather through the law we become conscious of sin." (Romans 3:20) If you recognize what happens is a reflection and take your opinion of it through the Epiphany Approach, you become more deeply conscious of your own particular sin. You get to see, hear, and understand the specific nature of your sin that the Holy Spirit desires you to work on. When you do this, the law is manifested inside your heart and responds in love; which is really why the law was created.

I Am Overwhelmed!

I looked around my house a while ago and it was totally disorganized. I had done some purging a few weeks before the holidays and all the stuff was still piled in the living room, but it was time to bring in the Christmas tree so I piled it all up in closets. Before I knew it, it was spring and I was jostling between warm weather clothing, winter clothing, and all the purged stuff from six months ago. Also, I hadn't been home seven straight days in three months so things were pretty grimy. I was going crazy [REFLECTION] searching almost two days for my voice recorder. I was so frustrated that I finally stopped for a moment and took in a good deep breath, and said out loud, "My outside is a reflection of my inside [OPINION]." Wow what an eye opener in full color. I knew immediately my thoughts inside of me were cluttered and unorganized and I was overwhelmed. God reminded me in that moment [EPIPHANY] that I had been saying, "I am overwhelmed," over and over, out loud, to whoever would listen for the last six weeks. It was in that moment that I remembered whining about being overwhelmed years back. I heard my mother's words as though she were standing right next to me. "I have found that, if I just start, before I know it, I am wrapping it up." Thank YOU, Lord for showing me [APPRECIATION]! My next thought was to the front hall closet [DECISION] and before I knew it (well, twenty-four hours later and with big help from my daughter) the whole apartment had been purged of the unwanted and was spic and span from top to bottom.

I sat right down afterward and wrote a couple of chapters. They just flowed out of me, not because my outside changed (although I have to admit it was lovely to be surrounded with clean order), but because my thoughts weren't cluttered. Please note that FIRST it was the thought that changed from "I am overwhelmed" to "I am tackling the front hall closet". The inside changed then the outside followed suit.

All things that happen can be processed following the same pattern. Someone declares a judgment. Go in. There's an epiphany, be thankful, and a pivotal decision follows.

A Bleeding Ulcer

An inmate came into class very upset over how a fellow inmate was being treated. He had a bleeding ulcer and was throwing up blood. The nurse just told him to take fewer ibuprofen. That was it. My student was furious over the nurse ignoring his friend. I explained that there is probably one area in his life, one place where he was ignoring something that needed his attention. And it could be serious. It's something that is draining his life blood out of him and that because he is so angry about it, I know it is something that is important. With the same intensity that he is angry over the nurse not taking care of his friends' situation, he is that intensely angry at himself for ignoring his own situation. He wouldn't share it with me, but we both knew he found what it was. I explained that he could preserve this situation by continuing to do the same thing or he could decide to do something different.

The Epiphany Approach Through Collective Experience

I went in to teach at the jail and requested a certain student to attend. The correction officer said, "She doesn't want to come."

I said, "Really, are you sure?"

"Yes," he replied. "She doesn't want to come."

I was so surprised. We had developed rapport and she had some real breakthroughs in my class.

As the rest of the inmate girls came in, before they had even sat down, they were questioning me as to why their cellmate wasn't allowed to come to class. I was immediately offended [REFLECTION]! The comment I made was, "HEY, HE DIDN'T TELL ME THE TRUTH! [OPINION]" One inmate said, "Oh, the CO's lie to everybody all the time." And another girl said, "Oh, they're so controlling!"

Those opinions were good fun! Here is why: this is an incredible example of how our outside is a reflection of our inside as a collective! We all experienced the same scenario, but we all had a different take on it, didn't we? The CO, in my opinion, did not tell me the truth. It took me fifteen minutes to discover where it was on the inside of me that I wasn't telling myself the truth. I was ignoring the truth. It was such a wonderful lesson.

While I was trying to figure out my issue, the girls were trying to figure out what their individual inside issue was. We all knew and had discussed instances where lying was a problem for the girl who recognized that the CO was lying. That was not a revelation. It really was a reflection of what was going on inside of her. You know the other girl who said, "Oh, those CO's! They just like to be in control." Well, guess who was the control freak in the group? We then went a step beyond!

The Root

Let's look at our liar first. Her job was to go in and discover the specific thing that she was lying to herself about, and to everybody else as well! Because the truth was going to set her free! She said, "When I wrote my mom, I told her I wasn't going to have anything to do with my old boyfriend and I was telling everyone how I was going to avoid him, but really I am lying to myself. In the back of my mind I know I am going to seek him out when I get out of here [EPIPHANY]." She couldn't do anything about what she was not consciously aware of. She had power now to choose [Preservation] or [Transformation].

Use Your Own Words

It was important for me to go right in and discover exactly what I was not being truthful to myself about. I didn't ask myself, "Where is it that I am lying to myself?" Those two sentences seem like they are the same thing, but not really. When you use your own personal words to go in, you will discover you. That is how you will find the CORE of the issue. If I were to use the other girl's words "Where is it that I am lying to myself," the answer would have been much harder to come by and I would have not discovered what God was trying to tell me.

I Am a Nag

I had the very big misfortune of having to ride in a truck for four hours without any way out of the situation, with a person I did not know very well, who smoked, on occasion I was told. Occasionally to this individual meant about every twenty minutes. I will have you know that I am a reformed smoker. I smoked Marlboro Reds for ten years and I really don't like secondhand smoke. As the time ticked slowly, mile marker after mile marker, I got mouthier and mouthier in my head. The sarcastic and snide remarks that were on the tip of my tongue were fierce. Exasperated, I stared out the window so mad there was probably smoke coming from my own nostrils. Every time the conversation would start up, I would think of another quick line I could whip that person to death with. Three and a half hours and a half a pack later I started to consider this parable God was showing me [REFLECTION]. Remember now, not a single nasty word left my lips regarding my disapproval of the cigarette smoke. I went in and asked God for help [COMMUNION]. I was horrified. I saw my ex-husband walking away from me with exasperated arms in the air saying, "You are such a nag!" I saw my children's faces looking at me with resentment! I AM A NAG [EPIPH-ANY]! I'm a sarcastic, whiny, nasty nag. What I thought was a big misfortune turned out to be one of the biggest blessings ever [APPRECIATION].

I called my children immediately and apologized [DECISION]. My son showed no mercy, "You mean you are just figuring that out now?" Susan said, "Yeah, Mom! I'm glad you get it now." I explained I was going to need some help and patience to change how I communicated with them. This was going to be like speaking a foreign language. I only knew of one way to communicate that I didn't like something and that I thought it should change and how I thought it should change. I must admit I sometimes slip back to my old ways, but I am persistent at making a conscious effort to not nag.

I had the most fun with my daughter shortly after my epiphany. The whole house was completely clean, picked up and organized. Until she left a candy bar wrapper on the large footstool in front of the couch. There it sat through the day and night. Now it was morning the next day. My head was crazy with solutions to my problem. I was about to burst over this stupid wrapper. I called her out to the living room still not knowing how I was going to get my message to her. We met next to the couch. I looked down at the wrapper and back up to her eyes where I caught her also glancing at the wrapper. And like a cork out of a bottle I exploded with "MADE YOU LOOK!" We both burst out laughing. I giggled all the while I watched her put the wrapper in the garbage. We were both happy with the simple experience [Transformation]. She didn't have to hear that nagging sound of my voice. I was triumphant in conquering my urge to do so. I was able to communicate what I wanted in a fun way without nagging at all! How cool is that?

How to "Handle" Someone

My daughter had a boyfriend who didn't really treat her very well [OPINION]. I even had a mom call me to report that he wasn't really treating her very well. I liked him enough as a person, he just had some relationship issues that didn't fare well for my daughter. I spoke to her about how I felt and made a couple of "suggestions." No real change took place. It really bothered me [REL-FECTION] and I was...well, I wasn't in a relationship. I couldn't figure out how that situation applied to me. I used my opinion and asked God [COMMUNION], "How is it that I am not treating me very well?" Then I realized [EPIPHANY] I hadn't been to the gym nor had I been eating very well! I understood I needed to treat me well! Thank you [APPRECIATION], Jesus, I know exactly what to do now [DECISION].

This situation with my daughter surfaced so that I could get a clue about ME. I began to make some changes in those areas. I started treating myself better [TRANS-FORMATION]. I didn't really sense any change in my daughter's situation. However, shortly thereafter I went to my class reunion and met a friend I dated a few times my senior year. (We are married now and after ten years we are still in the honeymoon phase!) He treats me so well! And the best part is that within three weeks of my class reunion my daughter broke up with that boy and began dating a real nice boy that treated her beautifully with kindness and respect! The other BEST PART is that I didn't have to wield my authority over her by controlling her every move or nagging her to death. You have seen examples where the parent forbids something and the kid is determined to have it. The problem just mushrooms into a catastrophe.

I work with the Law of Reflection instead. Countless women all over the world are wrecking their relationships with their husbands and children trying to get them to "do it their way" or to behave. They are pushing their loved ones right out of their lives and into the very scenarios that they are trying to protect them from.

He Ignores Me

He is ignoring me. I had to laugh at myself when I realized that. It was a two-fold problem. The moment I felt ignored I would go to the fridge or snack cupboard! Really what I was craving was companionship with my husband. The deeper I went in with God I realized that this whole time I was really desiring companionship with me. Me—a listener to my inner most places. Me—to join me in everything that I was doing. Doing the dishes, working on my business, running errands.

Do you see what I mean? The whole time I was doing these things, my mind wasn't hanging out with me, really. It was out in his business. My thoughts were on him. I would be saying things to myself like, "He went fishing without me," "He is all wrapped up in himself," "He never calls me until he needs something." I started consciously focusing my mind on what I was doing—feeling the warm bubbles in the dishwater. Hearing the water splash. Feeling the steering wheel in my hands. I would think of a time when we did go fishing together and a smile would creep across my lips. In that moment I was with him. In that moment I decided that I would take care of the inside of me and keep me in a place of contentment with my husband.

He started paying attention to me. I kept good feeling flowing between him and me and it connected us in a good way. If I would have harbored the negative emotion of being ignored by him, our conversations would have had a WALL between us of my yucky thoughts and feelings. We build these walls all the time and the longer we harbor these accusations and feelings the thicker, denser, wider, and taller that wall becomes, until all communication is severed.

I have showed you how we suffer. It is by looking outward. It is by keeping your mind focused on other people and what they do or do not do, all the while your happiness is but a moment away. It is inside your heart. Those people will keep showing up in your life, not because that is just the way it is, but because God loves you so much that He wants to show you how you are treating yourself on the inside so you can change that and, in turn, change your outside circumstances. You play a significant role in what you are about to experience.

The Intensity Is Always Reciprocal

A family member of mine emailed me this horrible email about how insensitive I am, what a bad mother I am, and how inconsiderate I am. It was filled with horrible, horrible things. I can tell you that ten years ago my response would have been Right Back at Her, if you know what I mean! I would have listed my response in the same fashion by pointing my finger back at her and the battle would have continued on and on.

You see, now I understand. Her words are coming from the inside of her. If she sees me, notices me being those things and it bothers her, it is because those things are actually happening on the inside of her. With as much intensity as she said, "YOU ARE SO INCONSIDER-ATE," with the same tone of voice she used, with the same belief in knowing that "Christine is inconsiderate," guess what I know about her? I know that she talks to herself with the same tone of voice, with the same words, and with the same intensity about herself. And so now I don't react to her tirades. I could not pour any more wrath upon her than she is already pouring out upon herself. When she is laying down for bed at night, when she is driving down the road, in her mind she is being very unkind to herself. Now what can I possibly respond with that would be of greater punishment than she is dishing out to her own self? Nothing. This is how I get to show up and be like Jesus.

Huge Red Flag

Another beautiful nugget to discover is that because she noticed those things about me, there is actually some truth to what she is saying! That is the real reason it drives us crazy. If someone notices (has an opinion) that I adamantly deny, that is a HUGE RED FLAG for me to know that there is something there for me to discover.

There Is Always Truth to Discover

For example, she said I was a bad mother. It was enticing to me to discover what the truth was about that for myself [RELFECTION]. I went in! I asked myself, "How is it that I am being a bad mom? [OPINION]" I sat with that question for a moment with the Lord, and then all of a sudden, I knew! I realized I hadn't spoken to my son in over two weeks [APPRECIATION]! We're not on a schedule or anything, but I usually speak to him every few days or so. Maybe even a week will go by, but this was too long! I called him immediately [DECISION]

[Transformation]! He was just walking out of class after finding out he got an A on an exam! Thank God I have learned to view my outside as a parable directly from God! If I had been all caught up in pointing my finger at her for saying those hurtful words to me, I would have missed the opportunity of speaking to my son at the perfect moment!

What I responded to her email was thank you. Thank you, for showing me, me. And I truly meant that. I was truly grateful that she pointed it out to me.

The Positive Side of the Mirror

It is not all doom and gloom with the Law of Reflection. Okay so something happens and you get upset over it or something happens and you are delighted over it. Well whatever it is, you are doing that on the inside of you. The groovy part of this lesson is that if you have someone in your life that is treating you really well and saying nice, kind words to you, and treating you well, guess what is on the inside of you!? YOU ARE BEING KIND AND WONDERFUL TO YOU and treating yourself really well! Everything that happens is a parable of what is happening on the inside of you based on the emotional pull or the emotional invocation of what you're feeling. Every single moment of every single day is a reflection of what you have going on inside of you. If, in your opinion, you are surrounded by people that are loving and considerate, or maybe FUN and carefree, then you are doing and being that to your own self.

Four Types of SHIFT Resulting from the Law of Reflection

Getting intimate with God and using the LOR as a tool to converse with Him will bring about tremendous shifts in your life. You will begin getting a lot more of the good stuff and a lot less of the yucky stuff showing up in your life. It is like math. The equation and the subsequent results can be proven over and over again.

Here are the four shifts that you will begin experiencing with regard to the parables, or people and situations you have a problem with, when you connect with the Lord:

1. They or it will stop doing what bugs you. For instance, if nagging was the issue and you stop nagging you, they will stop nagging you without you having tell them to stop.

2. They or it will drift away from you. For instance, their schedule will change or circumstances won't put you in proximity with each other.

3. You will drift away from them. Your situation or schedule will change causing you two to not be together or there won't be an opportunity for you to connect at the level that caused you stress.

4. The other thing that happens is that you two will continue to be together, however, they or it

will not bother you. At the very least you won't be bothered with the same intensity. "Hip, Hip Hooray!" It will be less troublesome. In other words, they will continue to do the thing that drove you crazy, but it won't drive you crazy anymore. One inmate described it this way: "He doesn't knock me off my square anymore." There just isn't a negative energy feeding frenzy!

These four results can be counted on like we can count on the sun coming up tomorrow.

It Can Get Worse—For a Bit

Using the Law of Reflection always produces a SHIFT, but it can take time for a complete elimination. Sometimes the very frustration you have been working on will intensify and get worse! Here is one scenario. You notice your husband is speaking to you with disdain. You exposed that disdain is operating inside of you by using how your husband showed up to show you that what you are seeing, hearing and feeling is a parable designed especially for you. After you have uncovered what God was trying to tell you and you begin to make the necessary inside changes, all heck breaks loose! You find that your husband really ramps up his disdain for you with greater intensity and frequency! It makes you think, "How can this be happening? It is getting worse!" You have exposed the "dirty rotten scoundrel" that has been stealing your joy! You've cut off the enemy's energy supply and it is madder than heck. But, keep going in, because it will begin to happen less frequently and less intensely! You see, you will at least begin to notice that you're not getting knocked off balance as much when your husband walks in the door. You begin to respond to him or the situation instead of reacting to it. Soon you will be able to pat yourself on the back; literally, praise yourself for changing. Your husband and kids will comment about the change they've noticed in you. You will be smiling and feel more content and satisfied. Your family will want to be with you. They will be attracted to you and you will want to be with them. You won't avoid them anymore! Disdain no longer runs your life because it has been exposed to the light. You know the real truth.

Sometimes It's Not an Exact Image

Some students will argue with me about the Law of Reflection because they can't make a connection to what they have going on in their life. For example, I had a client say, "My brother won't go get a job. But that can't be a problem that I have because, you see, I have a job. How is it that I can be doing that to me?"

Sometimes we have to build a little bridge. It is still a reflection but not a perfect reflection. Let's see how this works. So, their brother won't go get a job. Here is the question I ask: "How is it that you won't go get a job?" In other words, you need to get a job—or maybe a different job? This can be so funny because when I flip it around, they will have a revelation.

"Oh my gosh! I really hate my job. I am complaining about it all the time. I really need to get a new job! WOW, my brother's situation really is a parable for my own situation."

Let's look at another scenario my client could have had. "How is it that you need to get a job?" "I don't need to get a new job I love my job and I am making money. He is the one who needs to get a job."

I say, "Okay, yes that is absolutely true! AND what else is true? How is it that you need to get a different job? Maybe it is not the job you are making money from. What kind of job do you have that you need to stop doing or maybe change?" If my client would think it through, he may discover, "I need to get a new job from not nagging my brother about getting a new job."

Do you get this? The next time he runs into his brother, and the thought comes up that "Man, dude, you really need to get a job." He realizes that his new job is to not be the boss of his brother. He can now be a supportive friend to his brother instead of an oppressive nagger.

Basically, build the bridge and use what is happening in front of you to discover what is happening on the inside of you because that is what you can change. Can you make someone get a job? Can you make someone listen to you? You can't. What you can do is discover how your outside is a reflection of you. And then change that. The question you ask God is, "How is it exactly that I am doing that to me?"

If you are having trouble building the bridge, email me at lordsavemymarriage@gmail.com. I am available to connect with you to get on the other side of what is causing you the stress and frustration.

Sometimes It Keeps Happening

> *"I applied my heart to what I observed and*
> *learned a lesson from what I saw."*
> –Proverbs 24:32

This lesson is the core of what my message is. You can root out what is frustrating you. I think you have discovered that the root is inside of you. And the root is in the form of a thought or opinion. And the way to root it out is to first recognize the thought. For example, "Hey, that guy is really selfish.". Go find out what it is that you are keeping away from you that you really deserve. Go find it.

Everything that happens is a parable of what is going on inside of you.

If someone cuts you off while you are driving down the road. "Man, that guy just cut me off!" Well how is it exactly that you have just cut you off I used to have people pull out in front of me all the time. Each time someone would cut me off I would ask myself "How is it that I am cutting myself off?" And I would get a different answer each time based on what was going on in my life at the time. My answer might be one day, "Oh, I haven't prayed to God yet today and therefore I am cutting myself off from God." If I get cut off the next day, I ask the question and God's answer is that I should have called that guy back because by not calling him back I am cutting myself off from work. Things may keep happening, but it is to show you a different aspect of your life. How is it that I am still doing that to me?

Actually, now it is great to report that it rarely happens to me anymore. It seems that most of the time I have this free-flowing road in front of me, because my outside is a reflection of my inside.

Most of us were raised with parents that believed that if only their outside would change, then they'd be happy on the inside. That is how the world looks at things. God looks at things of the heart and now you know you can too, thereby changing your outside. You can transform your home from turmoil into peace regardless of how your husband shows up, or what he says in anger. You will no longer be sucked into arguing with him because you now know that nothing comes out of his mouth unless it is happening on the inside of him first. You are not his problem.

CHAPTER 9

Take a Hand

The last key is to use the keys. Some of these keys you've known all along. But why aren't you using them?

Support.

For every accomplishment I've had and difficult situation I've navigated, I've had support. When I was learning how to swim, it was my mom who was there, encouraging me and helping me to practice. When I was learning how to water ski, it was my dad, holding me up from under my arms, giving me pointers—keep your knees bent and arms locked straight, ski tips up, stay strong. You can do this! And sure enough, before long I was gliding on top of the water.

When I began to learn about Jesus, my sisters in Christ were there setting regular times for us to be in God's Word, showing me how to pray, sharing in the victory, and helping me to recognize the devil's ways.

I can't really find a time where I made any advances all on my own. I have countless stories of choosing to do things on my own. Rarely did they end well. Trying to handle my husband's drunken tirades by myself just resulted in having to handle my husband's drunken tirades, again, all by myself. Around and around I'd go where it would stop nobody knew. But God knew. I was scared, I mean, even though my husband was awful, it was familiar. Transformation was scary.

There are obstacles in the way of you having the desire of your heart - peace in your home from now on. One obstacle is thinking that just by reading this information and applying it a couple times you will be able to thrive amongst the oppression of his drunken rants, and immediately have the relationship you've always dreamed it would be.

Some of these concepts are brand new to you. To get them in your bones it will take practice. If you're not one of those self-starters that can take a concept and implement it into your everyday life and routine, then you'll need expert help. I mean, even if you grew up on God's Word, you were not taught how to apply it to change people by changing yourself in a practical way.

If you are like most people, you'll dabble in the easy keys and then soon forget them. A year from now you'll find this book dusty under your bed. Let's face it, if you could have transformed your marriage by reading a book, even the Bible, you probably would have done it by now. God wants us in relationships.

The other obstacle that blocks you from unlocking all the potential in your marriage is to invest in the right teacher. As I look around my office, I see two bookcases filled with books—spiritual self-help books. Most of them only gave me fleeting moments of epiphanies, but offered no lasting transformation. There are five books that led me to teachers that understood me. They were clear about what I wanted to accomplish and they challenged me, cheered for me, and got me unstuck. They called me out on my thought patterns and how I was handling things. They gave me the right tools I needed at just the right time and helped me to hear Jesus in my heart so he could use me to turn things around.

God always seemed to bring me just the right teacher who had already experienced the crap I was going through and figured out the best way to handle the problem just so I could be taught how. With help, I was shown not only how to avoid pitfalls, but how I could succeed way faster than doing it all on my own.

My teachers weren't always nice with sugar and spice either. They weren't in it to coddle me. They held me to the fire so that I got what I came for no matter what excuse I gave them. I am so grateful for them and their influence over my own transformation—my metanoia.

The most important aspect of investing in the right teacher is that they will help you get new tools in your routine on a consistent basis and help you through the pitfalls of resistance to change. Fear is such a show-stopper. You discovered here that you can actually change your husband, but first you have to use how he shows up and what he does in order to go in, commune with God, and make a decision. It is time for you to go in and decide.

You know this routine now. You can choose preservation Just keep doing the same thing you've been doing for years—living with that weekly ride on your husband's cyclical Ferris wheel of drinking, ranting, passing out, guilt-ridden turmoil trip that never seems to really ever end. Or you can choose transformation. I caution you, if you don't pick up the phone or get online and make an appointment with a qualified teacher or coach within the next fort-eight hours, you have chosen preservation without an expiration date. Preservation can last a lifetime. I just want you to be clear that doing nothing in this case proves preservation is what you most want at this time.

Sweetheart, you can take the next step. Jesus is with you, supporting you. I trust that God will present you with that perfect helper. I don't take on everyone who calls me. I do take on everyone's best interest with a discernment process that always leads to the best solution for the seeker, and it's not always to work with me. I know God will bring me exactly the right clients I am destined to work with.

I can speak with you personally about what your best path forward is for transforming your homelife with your alcoholic husband. I know your challenges, and no matter how alone you feel, I've either been through them myself or I've guided others. I know the way through. If you choose to sign up to speak to me, we will work to clarify a step-by-step game plan to make your very best attempt to transforming your marriage and bringing it to a place that feels good again, filling your home with peace and love regardless of how your alcoholic husband shows up.

CHAPTER 10

Sending Forth

Y ou've learned a lot in this book and from God's Word.

Take a big deep breath in and out. Call on the name of Jesus. Ask Him for what you need, what you need to do now. Will this book go on your bookshelf with all the other books you've purchased that only gave you a fleeting result before you went searching for the next thing that would ease the pain? There are so many things that will stop you from getting the peace in your home you've been praying for. Reading a book one time is not going to transform your life or your husband.

Practicing—real time—in calling on the name of Jesus will build your trust. Seeing Him work miracles right in front of you at your command of His name will build a deep reliable faith in Him. Getting your most valuable ingredient in your body not only honors Him for the very breath you've been given, but it physically gets your very braincells connected to God. You can hear Him, and see Him, and sense His leading.

Genesis was written to you. The very first thing He wanted you to know is what to do about a situation—hover over it. Take it all in. Be creative. You have been made in the image of God. Speak out what it is you want, not what you do not want.

God created us with seven silent forms of language. When we speak each other's dominant silent language, we are telling them we love them or hate them. What kind of relationship do you want? You hold the keys.

With the Law of Reflection, you now know that the drama on the outside of you is the drama going on inside of you, at least metaphorically. When you recognize the reflection, you have power to change it and the people around you with the Epiphany Approach. It's how you can intimately connect with the Lord to discover yourself through the person He happens to have in front of you! If you truly don't want that drama any more, the only way, and I mean the only way, is to go in and ask Jesus how is it that you are doing that very same thing to your own self. And then stop doing that. The drama will dissipate.

The best part of all these keys is that Jesus is still teaching you with parables because you hear Him and see Him. You have witnessed the power in knowing this fact. Your jaw has dropped at the epiphany of knowing that God was speaking directly to you with what was in front of you. Use this knowledge wisely. Get it in your bones. Seek out the helping hand that can show you how to get peace in your home. You weren't meant to do it alone.

My Prayer for You

Lord, please meet my friend where she is at right now. Take her hand. Help her to see you crystal clear, to hear you clear as a bell, and to choose transformation. Completely disintegrate her paralyzing fear. Lord, I put a hedge of protection around her mind, her home, and around her family. Help her, Father, as she struggles with worry over how her husband might hit his bottom, or that he never will. Help her to trust you, and to be able to use these tools to get closer to you. I pray that you renew her mind. Lord, I acknowledge her sadness and the loneliness she feels and I ask you to lift it from her countenance and replace it with your presence. Calm her husband's anger, and calm her anger, Lord. Fill her every cell with your wisdom for healing, prosper her, expand her territory. It is all for you, Lord. When her husband shows his nasty side, bring to her mind these tools, heal him of his drinking problem, and fill their home with your loving peace. Thank you, Jesus, for dying for our sins so that we could be with You in Your throne room any time we want. Thank You for Your Holy Spirit who lives in us and guides us. You are Holy, Lord. You are Holy, Awesome, and Mighty. We love You. Amen.

Acknowledgements

This book has been a long time in the making and without Angela Lauria, and the whole TAI team this book would still be in my head and weighing on my shoulders. Todd Hunter, our conversations were pivotal. Thank you so much. Thank you as well to David Hancock and the Morgan James Publishing team for helping me bring this book to print.

To my husband, Brian, I wish there was a word that means I love you, but it means love that expands past all the galaxies God ever made because that is how much I love you. Thank you for cherishing all of me. I think you are super amazing for supporting this book even though you know that people will automatically think you are the husband who treated me so badly.

To my Ladies Bible Study Ladies, Mindy Kruzel, Cindy Kramer, Kelli Mouseau, and Sue Tock, who have supported my journey through the tears and worries and discernment process. You have been there for me, studying, loving, and praying for me. Your friendship and encouragement have nurtured my heart. Love you.

To Dawn Bindschatel, who always knew this book would be written one day! Your support, friendship, and love mean the world to me. You are the BEST!

To my first husband, I am so grateful to you because without our relationship being the way it was, I would not know Jesus or God's Word as intimately as I do. I wouldn't be helping my Christian Sisters get peace in their homes.

Thank You

Thank you so much for reading through your survival guide. The fact that you've gotten to this point in the book tells me something important about you. You're ready. You are ready to have your husband meet Jesus living inside you, instead of you. You're ready to experience peace in your home and in your heart no matter how he shows up.

To support you in your communication with your husband, I created The Specular Test to determine what attributes God has given your husband that were created just for *you* to experience.

www.christianwomansguide.com/ty

They will answer a few questions and when they submit them those answers will be used to send them an email with the results.

About the Author

Christine Lennard Folk is the founder of Epiphany Approach. As she struggled to not be codependent of her husband, she kept connected to God, begging Him to intervene, all the while keeping her nose in the Bible searching for answers about how to cope with an alcoholic husband and stay married because, for her, divorce was not an option.

Jesus brought her support, circumstances, and experiences that led to the creation of the Seven Silent Languages and the Epiphany Approach—communication keys that transform hearts and minds regardless of the other person. She knew they worked to transform her home of turmoil into a place of peace. Christine began her career teaching these stress relieving techniques to inmates in Northern Michigan county jails. She now puts all her effort into helping her Christian sisters who are where she once was. Her mission is to show as many wives of alcoholic husbands as possible how to get peace and solace in their homes. Christine speaks to Christian women's organizations and works one-on-one with Christian women who also desire to stay married to the man they love, despite his alcoholism. Jesus showed her that the reason she went through the abyss and back was to help you to be like Jesus so that when the alcoholic side of your husband shows up, you have the composure and knowledge to defuse the situation.

Christine is a wife, grandmother, and mother of four grown children. One of her most favorite things to do is watch the Epiphany come over her clients! Priceless!

9 781642 797770